Prepare for Departure

A GUIDE TO MAKING THE MOST OF YOUR STUDY ABROAD EXPERIENCE

SHELLEY STORY

But you are the only person alive who has sole custody of your life. Your particular life. Your entire life.

-Anna Quindlen

Contents

Preface

I had the rare fortune to spend nine years, from 2006 to 2015, living in Florence, Italy, and working with hundreds of American students who chose the capital of Tuscany as their study abroad destination for a summer term, a semester, or an academic year (and in a few cases, more than one of those). Over the course of those nine years, I learned so much about how students prepared — or didn't — to study abroad, and what events, situations, and circumstances impacted the quality of their experience for better and worse. My goal as a student development staffer was always to share as much of what I had learned as possible, and to challenge students as best I knew how, to help them get the most out of their term abroad.

This book is a continuation of that quest. Although I no longer live in Florence and am no longer responsible for managing a study abroad program, I hope that by sharing what I learned, I can continue to help students thrive while abroad.

The contents of this book are derived from my lived experience as an American in Italy, as an educator supporting American students as they spent time in Italy, and as an administrator who traveled with those students, throughout and beyond Europe (an average of ten days out of every month of those nine years). I write from those perspectives, so the book appeals — literally — to American students considering or planning to study abroad in Europe. Specifics aside, I believe this book could also be helpful to anyone planning to travel or move to a country other than their home country, especially for the first time. So, if you aren't from the U.S., or you aren't headed to

Europe, you'll still find much of this text useful; I think you'll be able to recognize what applies to your circumstances directly, and what does not will at least have you asking some good questions.

If you are from the U.S. **and** headed to Europe, I hope you'll feel like this book was written specifically for you. It was.

Housekeeping

Throughout the book, you'll see references to "the workbook." This is a 14-page PDF document available at no additional charge to readers of this book. It contains supplemental information that can help you put some of the book's concepts into practice. Material in the workbook is there — instead of in the book — because most of it is designed to be printed out and scribbled on.

To get your copy, go to shelleystory.com/workbook.

Introduction

If you're reading these words, chances are you have some relationship to study abroad, from "my interest is piqued" to "I'm leaving next week and don't know if I'm ready!" Or, maybe you're the parent or loved one (or study abroad or academic advisor) to a student who wants to study abroad. Either way, I hope you'll find value in this book.

In some regards, it's probably exactly what you expect from a resource intending to make a student's study abroad experience richer, better, smoother. There's a chapter on safety and security, one on health and wellness, one on basic skills you need to get around on your own. But the most comprehensive travel guide couldn't identify every possible scenario a student might face while abroad. Even if it could, it's impractical to stop in the middle of life and consult your book for an answer. As an educator, I don't believe that you need answers to every question; rather, you need the ability and resourcefulness to find answers as the questions arise. I've spent twenty years working with college students and seeing what challenges they face, how they learn, how they overcome (or succumb to) obstacles. The influence of that knowledge and experience is evident in these pages.

I've tried to strike a balance between specific, practical information and the kind of guidance and advice you'd get from a trusted family friend who's got a lot of experience with something you're just embarking on. I've written in a conversational tone, by design. This book is about life — making the most of an opportunity, being open to possibility, and just enjoying the heck out of each moment. It's not academic, not research-based (unless you count my nine years and

2000+ students abroad as research), and not meant to be a difficult read. It's full of *my* opinions and *my* perspectives, which are a vehicle of expression for my deep desire that everyone who studies abroad plays all out and has the best experience possible *for them*.

The assertion of this book is this: your best experience begins with quality preparation, and that preparation is made up of not just *planning*, but also of *practice* and *process*. You'll find support for all three here, and I start big, with process. Don't let that scare you! It's a thread that runs through the entire book, and I promise that if you take the time to consider the process questions, your term abroad will be a powerful springboard for a life full of exploration, adventure, and openness to diverse experiences. When you're grounded in who you are and what you want, you can create an experience that is perfectly designed for you, by you. Let's get started!

CHAPTER 1

The First Step of a Lifelong Journey

You've decided to study abroad in Europe. Congratulations! You're embarking on a journey that will introduce you to new cities, countries, cultures, food and drink, attitudes, beliefs, customs, and of course, people. You're also embarking on a journey that will introduce you to parts of *yourself* you might never

To be yourself in a world that is constantly trying to make you something else is the greatest accomplishment.
-Ralph Waldo Emerson

have met otherwise. How you meet these new ideas, these new people, and this new you, will depend heavily on your preparation. This book is designed to help prepare you for many of the details of daily life that might feel surprising or unsettling, so that you spend more of your time appreciating and absorbing the environment around you, and less time struggling with unfamiliar systems and practices. But it's also designed to help you discern, define, and keep focused on what you really want out of your time abroad.

In this chapter, I'll cover some of the internal and external preparation you can do to increase your chances of having a smooth transition to your destination abroad, and reduce the possibility of realizing halfway through your stay that you've been letting lack of clarity or intimidation run your schedule.

You probably feel like you've already done a lot of planning. You had to decide where you'd study — both where in the world and at which institution — make sure that your credits would transfer, and be confident that there would be enough "meaningful" classes available for you to keep making progress toward your degree (or, if not, decide that the experience was worth it anyway). You had to figure out your finances — what scholarships or aid would transfer, how different the cost of studying abroad would be from a semester or year at your home university, how much money you'd need in the bank for visa purposes and for expenses while abroad, how you'd pay for the airfare. You might have even already worked on a plan for your family or friends to visit you while you're away, or for what trips you might take within Europe from your study abroad home-base, or for how you'd stay connected with your family and friends. So, you might be thinking, "I've been planning for months! I'm done with planning now!" You might instead be thinking, "Wow, I haven't done half of this stuff yet, and now I'm overwhelmed." Whether you've already planned everything you can think of, or you're just getting started on the road to studying abroad, this book can help you. **That's because planning is just one part of preparing to live and study abroad.** You can — and should — plan where to go, what to pack, which classes to take, where you'll live, how you'll pay for it. But there are many other things you can — and, I believe, should — do to **prepare for the experience of living abroad.** I'm talking about both the physical sphere and the emotional/intellectual sphere.

What do you really want from your time abroad? What do you know about the country and culture where you'll be a guest (and a foreigner)? What is the condition of your health, and how will that support or hinder your achieving your goals? What skills do you have that will support your experience? In what areas do you feel less competent, and believe you'd be well served to feel more capable?

In my experience, developing a clear understanding of your own hopes and expectations for yourself and your study abroad experience is the single factor that can have the greatest positive impact on your total experience abroad. While you are sure to have some fantastic experiences whether you prepare well or not, taking the time to prepare can both enhance your overall experience and make your time abroad feel packed with value, and connected to your values, from the moment your flight takes off.

GETTING TO KNOW YOURSELF

Before you can establish a clear set of expectations and goals for your time abroad, it's important to have a good understanding of — and an ability to acknowledge — who you are. This may sound simple, but can actually be a pretty difficult exercise in today's fast-paced, always-on, connected-electronically-but-otherwise-not-so-much world.

Going abroad is similar, in some ways, to leaving home and going off to college. Think back to the anticipation, nervousness, and excitement you felt as you were getting ready to start your life as an independent adult. You're probably feeling some of those same emotions now, as you prepare to start over yet again, this time with even more independence. It can be very helpful to reflect on that earlier major transition to inform how you approach the one that's now ahead of you.

The college years are a time when you can re-evaluate the circumstances and expectations that might have previously guided your habits and lifestyle. Your parents, your siblings, your friend groups, your teachers, your community or church leaders — all of these people likely played important roles in shaping your activities, your beliefs, your habits, your likes and dislikes, even your speech patterns! When you left the environment in which those people had a daily influence in your life, you might have felt an overwhelming sense of freedom, like you had the chance to "redefine" yourself. Or, you might have felt homesick or a little lost, not sure who to turn to when you wanted guidance or advice. Chances are, you felt a little bit of both. But soon enough, you adjusted to your new community, which in turn, also influenced and helped to shape your activities, beliefs, and habits.

So, while you are still YOU, there might be things you say, activities you participate in, choices you make (whether it's how much to drink on Friday night or what you'll major in)... that you choose out of a sense of obligation, or because you got outvoted among your friends, or wanted to avoid conflict, or any other of dozens of reasons why we all do things that we're not 100% excited about or that don't align with our true selves.

If you give yourself the time and space, your term abroad can be a period when you get really clear about who you are, what you want, what you're willing to work for, and what it's time to give up (because you've been doing it for any reason other than it's exactly what *you* want to do). But I want to be straightforward in saying that you'll probably face lots of challenges during this time in your life. Facing these challenges and trying to figure out who you are and what you really want at the same time can be daunting. It can also be one of the most powerful experiences you'll have in your lifetime. These questions — **who am I? what do I want?** — are both basic and exceptionally complicated. All of those influences I mentioned earlier impact who you think you are and what you think you want. But there are so many other influences — the culture you grow up in, the media you're exposed to, the education you have access to, the people in your environment (even the ones you don't know personally), and so many more. So, who are you? What do you want? How do you know that's really what you want, and not what someone/something else taught you to want? What is important to you? What do you value most? It is with clear acknowledgment of the irony of it that I'll sometimes refer to these questions as the "Basic Questions." So let me repeat that **facing the challenges that will arise during your time abroad and trying to figure out who you are and what you really want at the same time can be daunting. It can also be one of the most powerful experiences you'll have in your lifetime.**

And, by spending some time thinking about and clarifying the Basic Questions for yourself before you depart, you'll give yourself a solid foundation from which to make any decisions, face any hurdles, and continue to hone and strengthen your answers to the Basic Questions.

Who am I?

What do I want?

What is important to me?

What do I value?

The answers to these questions are, as I just outlined, harder to discover and define than you might think they should be. That's okay. You'll probably spend most of your life revising and refining your answers. What's important is that you start thinking about the questions.

There are thousands of books to guide you through various niches of self-discovery and self-development. You can follow a process derived from religious teachings, or specific schools of psychological thought, or even modeled after particular fictional characters. If one of these methods speaks to you, or if you're already really interested in self-development, feel free to buy/borrow/check out as many books as hold your interest. Every additional input can assist you in answering the Basic Questions more fully, or from a different perspective.

If you're not interested in reading so much, though, you can still begin to figure out your answers to these questions in several ways:

BE MINDFUL OF YOUR DAILY ACTIONS AND CHOICES.

If I were to ask you, "what do you value most in life?" your answer might include things like *family*, *meaningful friendships*, *faith*, *my health*, *love*, or *financial security*. But if I then asked you to keep track of everything you do for a week, down to the half hour, and you looked back on that log of your time after seven days, I'd be willing to bet that you'd find you spend a lot of your waking time — maybe even up to half of it — doing things that don't support what you say you value. Simply reminding yourself of what's important to you at the beginning of each day can help you remain attentive to your choices and how they support (or don't support) your goals and values.

ASK YOURSELF SOME QUESTIONS THAT STRIP AWAY THE INFLUENCE OF OTHERS.

Spend a little bit of time each day thinking about hypothetical situations that would allow your true self to be more visible. The possibilities are endless, but here are some to get you started:

- Imagine your life as a movie of your life, where you are both an actor playing yourself, and the director. In what situations would the director-you tell you that you're not being true to your character? What would director-you have you do or say instead?

- If you were to transfer to another college in another town, and you had an entire semester and unlimited funds to visit colleges under consideration, what qualities would you look for in the colleges, communities, and potential friends you'd choose? As a new person in that community, what behaviors and habits would you want to be known for immediately? Which of your current habits or behaviors would you leave behind?

- Think of someone you admire and would like to emulate. What are the qualities you admire in that person? How might you develop more of those qualities in yourself?

- If you were to found a company, non-profit organization, or community of some kind, what kinds of rules would you put in place? What kinds of qualities would you look for in the people who would contribute to the organization?

The common thread among these questions, you'll notice, is that **you** are in charge. You get to start something new and choose who to be and how to be. Your answers will be great clues to who you are and what you really want.

NOTICE WHEN YOU'RE OFF TRACK.

If you find yourself feeling uncomfortable, either physically or emotionally, stop and ask yourself what might be the source of the discomfort. Have you used your time and energy in ways that don't support your true interests and desires? How can you change that?

JUST ASK THE QUESTIONS.

Try asking yourself each morning when you wake up and each night before you sleep: "Who am I?" See what responses come up, how they are similar or change over time. And try asking yourself, before each decision (whether it's as simple as what to do next in your day or as significant as whether to start or end a relationship), "What do I really want?" These two simple practices can make a quick and substantial contribution to your understanding of who you are and what you want, and to your actions supporting your identity.

WHY DOES ALL THIS MATTER?

At this point, you might be thinking, "I thought this book was going to help me prepare for my study abroad experience! Why are you trying to have me figure out who I am?" It's a valid question. And I've got an answer for you.

Over the nine years I spent working with college students while they studied abroad in Europe, I heard versions of the same story from hundreds of different people:

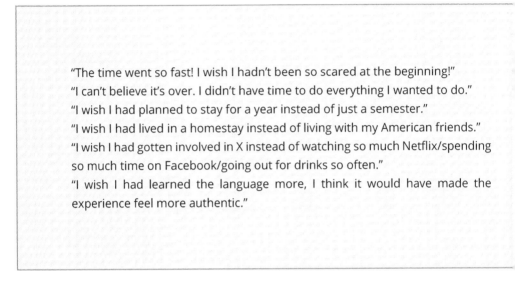

"The time went so fast! I wish I hadn't been so scared at the beginning!"

"I can't believe it's over. I didn't have time to do everything I wanted to do."

"I wish I had planned to stay for a year instead of just a semester."

"I wish I had lived in a homestay instead of living with my American friends."

"I wish I had gotten involved in X instead of watching so much Netflix/spending so much time on Facebook/going out for drinks so often."

"I wish I had learned the language more, I think it would have made the experience feel more authentic."

The examples could go on and on. But the underlying issue is clear: students often neglect to prepare fully (physically, mentally, and emotionally) for the study abroad experience.

So they spend the first few weeks staying at home, afraid to interact with anyone outside their school or program.

Or they spend the first few weeks going everywhere-all-the-time, and end up exhausted and sick, unable to enjoy the experience.

They don't learn the language because "everyone speaks English," and don't realize until it's too late what they've missed out on.

They let fear, or boredom, or lack of focus, or homesickness guide their daily activities, and suddenly their precious time abroad is over.

These potential regrets can be avoided, if you take the time to determine what you really want *in life* and how that translates to what you really want *in your study abroad experience*. The list of desired outcomes will be different for each person, so there are no right answers. But there are right answers **for you**.

As you build a list of answers to the Basic Questions, you'll also be building a reference list to help you as you make decisions while abroad. And as you learn to be mindful of your daily actions and choices, you'll be creating a habit that will serve you well while abroad.

A FEW MORE QUESTIONS

Once you've got a good start on those Basic Questions, you can begin to think more specifically about your style and preferences as they relate to travel. With the foundations of

- Who am I?
- What do I want?
- What is important to me?
- What do I value?

in place, it's time to think about questions like:

- What kind of traveler am I?
- What are my boundaries regarding meeting and developing relationships with others?
- What are my limits regarding participation in high-risk activities?
- What hobbies or interests from my "normal" life do I want to pursue while traveling, if any?
- How will I handle situations in which my own safety or the safety of others with me feels at risk?
- Are there activities or interests I'll pursue while abroad that I wouldn't while at home? If so, why? And what are they?

Let's take a deeper dive into some of these questions.

WHAT KIND OF TRAVELER ARE YOU?

If you've been on vacation for more than a few days at a time with other people (friends or family or both), you've probably noticed that after the first few days, the newness seems to wear off. Even though it's supposed to be an enjoyable experience where everyone gets to have fun and feel free, people start to get grumpy. This might occur because travelers come in different models, and if you put them all together into the same vacation schedule, it's probably not going to work for all of them at the same time. Some travelers prefer to have full days with a precise itinerary that guides them minute by minute from morning until evening; others want to wake up without an alarm, hit the streets, and follow their eyes (or nose or stomach) wherever they lead.

Before you go abroad, and certainly before you plan shorter trips from your home-base abroad, it's helpful to think about what kind of traveler you are and what plans and tools will best serve you.

Overview

The overview traveler is likely to have a 300-page guidebook in her carry-on, and books a guided tour or two when visiting a new place, to make sure she doesn't miss any of the major sights. She's unlikely to stray from the beaten path, and will choose destinations and itineraries based on what's most popular among people in her demographic. She's looking for an interesting, new experience, with a focus on safety, comfort, and "hitting the highlights."

The Singular Pursuit

The traveler who is in a singular pursuit has a love greater than the travel itself; the travel is just a way of getting access to more of what he loves. His passion might be for wine, or ice climbing, or modern art, but whatever it is, he'll go to the destinations where his passion can be experienced in a new way or in a new setting or at a different level. He's less interested in the standard local attractions, but deeply appreciates even the most subtle differences he can find related to his pursuit in new locales.

Sponge

The sponge just wants to soak it all in. She could be happy spending hours at an outdoor cafe, people-watching, sipping a lovely beverage, and engaging with the locals when approached. She experiences a new place most happily by listening to the language, watching the way locals interact, noticing their patterns, and maybe taking it all down in her journal or sketchbook. She might return from Florence without having seen the David, but she'll be able to tell you all about the colors, accents, tastes, and smells.

Schedule-Master

The schedule-master believes that every moment spent sleeping is a moment wasted! They've got a plan for each day, including exactly how long they'll spend at each museum, which restaurants they'll choose for meal breaks (where they also know which dishes are most recommended by at least three different sources), and what path they'll walk from point A to point B. The goal is to squeeze in as much exposure to the destination and its attractions as possible during the time they have available.

Checklist

The checklist traveler could also be called the "Instagram" traveler. She's interested in too many different things to spend hours focused on just one. She's not so interested in the history of the Eiffel Tower's construction, but she wants to see it and snap a photo or two. She'll pop into the most important museum to see the most well-known pieces, but she won't spend half a day there. She wants to taste all the local specialties, see the monuments, cruise the shopping street, and find the nightlife because, hey, when's the next time she'll get to dance 'til 2:00AM in Paris again? She's also likely to plan a 10-day trip that covers at least three countries; getting exposure to a few different places is more appealing to her than deep-diving into one.

Crowdsourcer

The crowdsourcer is the traveler who, two days before departure, posts something on Facebook like "Hey! I'll be in Barcelona for 72 hours this weekend. Give me your best tips... go!" He's looking for recommendations of all sorts, and wants to evaluate them based on how they sound as well as who's offering them. He wants a combination of the traditional and the quirky, the famous landmarks and the hidden gems. He wants to create his own experience with some planning, but with room for spontaneity as well.

Solo or Social? No matter your travel style, you'll probably also have a preference regarding whether you travel alone, with just one or two others, or in a big group. If you haven't traveled on your own before, it will probably feel safer to travel with a few others at first. When you're traveling in a group, it's important — for everyone's happiness — to talk about your travel styles before you depart. You won't all have the same style. So setting expectations in advance will make the trip more comfortable for everyone. For example, if you're a sponge, you might tell your friends that your idea of getting to know a place involves a lot of people-watching and soaking up the environment. So if they're really keen to visit a particular historical site, you might opt out of that half-day so that you can get your sponge time.

If you're traveling in a big group (more than six people), consider identifying pairs or subgroups that have similar interests and travel styles. The practicalities of moving a dozen people around by train (for example), are much more difficult and frustrating than when you're two or three. There's also a social dynamic in which the strongest personalities (or the most impatient, or those most willing to speak up) end up directing the activities of the whole group for the entire trip, and in the end, some group members feel disempowered while others feel responsible for the entire group's happiness (or lack thereof). In smaller groups, it's easier for everyone to express their wishes.

As you become a more confident traveler, you may find that you enjoy traveling alone. It offers a lot of freedom and flexibility; you don't have to worry about coordinating schedules or restaurant choices or departure times with anyone else. If you do choose to travel alone, be sure to leave your travel plans and your contact information with someone at your study abroad home-base (a friend, host family member, or local school administrator), in case of emergency.

Unsure of Your Travel Style?

You might not yet know what kind of traveler you are. You might be a blend of several of these types. Or you might think you're one type and discover over the course of your time abroad that your style is changing. It's all okay. What's most important is that you pay attention to the style of travel that inspires you most, and allow yourself to be that kind of traveler. No one's definition of what makes a good day abroad matters but yours.

KNOW YOUR LIMITS

You're getting to know yourself and your travel style. Now it's time to know your limits.

I've once compared going abroad to going off to college for the first time, and the comparison merits revisiting here. When you left home to go to college, you suddenly had the complete freedom and responsibility to make every little decision without anyone else's input (no micromanaging, but also no micro-help!). You had to decide whom to befriend and whom to avoid, what risks were worth taking and what was beyond your comfort level, when to ask for help and when to handle things yourself.

All of those choices will now be presented to you again — over and over — in a culture that isn't your own, in a language in which you're not likely fluent, in a place that isn't your home. What's more, your typical resources for help (your parents, family, or friends) will be time zones away, and also won't have a cultural context from which to give advice.

How will you respond?

When you'll be called on frequently to make choices involving your own well-being, your safety, and the safety of others around you, you'll be in the best position to make those choices if you've thought about them ahead of time, and decided on your own boundaries.

For example, meeting local people is an important and meaningful part of the experience abroad. If you spent a semester in Rome and didn't get to know a single Roman, you'd be missing out on a fundamental component of what it means to live in Rome, right? At the same time, if you're unfamiliar with the city and the language, you're more vulnerable to anyone who might have ill intentions (or even just be reckless). So how do you find and mingle with the locals and at the same time ensure that you'll feel safe?

The answer is different for each person. For some, it might mean only meeting locals at specific types of events, like art showings or organized happy hours designed for locals and visitors to meet. For others, it might mean never giving out more information than a first name and temporary phone number. For others, it might mean building up trust over multiple meetings and including others in those meetings. It matters less where your boundaries are, and more that you *know* where they are and realize when you're getting close to them. If you're tempted to cross those boundaries, you'll have a conversation with yourself to remind yourself why they exist in the first place, and then be better able to respect them, or perhaps move them, but with intention rather than on impulse.

Some other scenarios and questions that you might consider before they actually materialize:

Scenario: Soon after your arrival in your destination, your fellow students develop a habit of going out together nightly. Not knowing anyone other than your classmates, you join them.

Questions:

- How would spending all of your social time and energy with fellow students align with your goals and intentions for your experience abroad?

- Is the social safety created by the group positive, negative, or neutral?

- What would you gain by spending so much time with your peers? What would you be missing out on?

Scenario: You're an enthusiastic guitarist [or insert your favorite hobby here] and, at home, you play every day. You're trying to decide whether to bring your guitar with you, or use the time you'd normally spend playing on other things while abroad.

Questions:

- What role does your hobby play in your life? What qualities does it bring to your day?

- Are those qualities you'll need or want in your life while you're abroad? Are there other ways you could access them?

- Would playing the guitar [engaging in your hobby] daily support your goals for your time abroad, or detract from them?

Scenario: A group of friends is planning a weekend trip in which they'll participate in high-risk activities — skydiving, canyon jumping, bungee jumping, etc. You're invited to join them.

Questions:

- How would this kind of trip connect to your goals for your experience abroad?
- What appeals to you about participating? Is it more about being part of the group, or the adventuresome experience itself?
- How would you handle an injury or trauma to yourself or someone in your group?

Scenario: You're at a bar with one other friend, and that friend decides to go home with someone they met at the bar.

Questions:

- Do you believe it's your responsibility to convince the friend not to go home with the new acquaintance? Do you know enough about your friend to make that judgment call?
- Do the answers change if you believe your friend is drunk?
- If you're left to get home by yourself, how do you do that most safely?

STAYING ON YOUR PATH

Before we get to the nuts-and-bolts specifics, I have a few recommendations to help you stay connected to your values, identity, and goals for your study abroad experience.

NAME AND DISPLAY YOUR VALUES

Although you may later revise and refine it, do make an actual list of the values most important to you. If you don't know how to get started, see the Values Clarification exercise in the workbook. Once you have a list of your most dearly-held values, save it in some way that will have you interacting with it or reminded of it often. If you keep a paper calendar, write it in the inside front cover. If you carry a cell phone or tablet, make a wallpaper of the value words. Write them on a piece of paper you'll keep in your wallet, or tape them to the inside of your guitar case. However you do it, put them in a place where you'll be in touch with them frequently. Seeing the values you chose and affirmed will help keep them in the forefront of your mind as you face unknown terrain.

COMPLETE A TIME LOG

After the first few days you're abroad, when you've begun to settle in to a routine, complete a time log. You can use the one provided in the workbook, or keep track in your own calendar. Record how you spend your time for a week or so. Remember: it's not a planning calendar, so don't fill it out until the time has actually passed. Record what you did, not what you intended to do. After about a week, spend a few minutes looking over how you spent your time. It's a good idea to have your value list for reference. How do the values you say you embrace match up with the way you spend your time? What changes are you inspired to make? What activities and choices are well aligned with your values and will you continue?

COMMIT TO A WEEKLY CHECK-IN

Throughout your time abroad, make a practice of checking in each week so you'll be conscious of whether you're on track with your goals, making choices that support what you really want out of the experience. Again, you can either use the worksheet provided, or write in your own calendar or journal. Checking in consistently ensures you won't wake up one morning and feel like your term abroad is almost over and your goals and experiences haven't met your expectations.

KEEP A JOURNAL

You might already be accustomed to journaling and plan to do it anyway. If so, that's great! If not, think outside the box when it comes to journaling. You can do it however you want to. You can write just one sentence at the beginning or end of each day. You can journal through drawings, sketches, poetry or prose. You can journal on scraps of paper. You can make notes about your thoughts and experiences on a map of the place where they happened. No matter what form your journal takes, it's a way to record the intense development that's going on in you while you're abroad. Some of that development may not be obvious to you as it's happening, so it's helpful to keep track of it and be able to look back a few weeks later, with a different perspective. Journaling will also help you see your progress toward your goals, and celebrate when you're creating the experience you want.

In the next few chapters, I'll give you much more specific information about living and studying abroad. Knowing what to pack, how to save money, and what to do in an emergency are important. But I firmly believe that we've already laid the foundation of the best possible preparation you can do for your study abroad experience. If you're actively uncovering answers to the questions:

• who am I?

• what do I want from this experience?

• what are my values?

• what kind of traveler am I?

• where are my boundaries?

then it won't matter if you forget to pack your money belt. The quality of your time abroad will be infinitely enhanced by your mental and emotional preparation, because from day one, you'll be choosing, each moment, the paths that support exactly what you want from the experience.

CHAPTER 2

Pre-Departure

If this book found its way to you with fortuitous timing, you're probably in the pre-departure phase, whether your travel is days, months, or years away. You can benefit from considering the following

A journey of a thousand miles begins with a single step.
-Lao Tzu

categories as you prepare to study abroad; some may be more or less relevant to you, depending on your circumstances and the resources already available to you.

This chapter will help you "get your house in order" before departure, pointing out resources to help you with planning your term abroad, and giving you some practical advice about what to pack and where you might need to close some loops before leaving the country.

STUDY ABROAD OFFICE

If you're a current student at a university or college in the U.S., the first stop on your study abroad adventure should be your institution's study abroad office. It may go by a different name (like international education, or center for global citizens, or something specifically creative and unique to your school, like "Bears Abroad"), but without a doubt, your school has at least a staff member — and more likely, an office full of them — dedicated to helping you explore your options and implement a plan. The value of the services provided by your study abroad office cannot be overstated. These are people who have already advised students who were in a situation most similar to yours. Before you arrived, they had surely helped dozens or hundreds or thousands of students who were charting a course like you are now.

Take advantage of all the services your study abroad office has on offer. These may include:

- Individual advising appointments
- Academic advisors with a study abroad focus
- A resource library
- Questionnaires or formulas to help you find the best study abroad program for you
- Social programs where you can meet other students who studied abroad and learn directly from their experience
- A mentor program in which a student who has completed the same program you're interested in walks you through the process
- Group meetings of students heading out on the same program or to the same country
- Language or cultural houses related to your destination
- Assistance with processing and submitting visa applications
- Assistance with meeting the requirements of the sponsoring institution (if your program is not "owned" by your own school)

All of these services and more may be available from your study abroad office. At the same time, know that as more and more American students go abroad to more and more diverse locations, and as U.S. institutions continue to attract international students from all over the world, these study abroad offices may be less able to give you as much one-on-one, personal advice or attention as you need. Remember, while this is your one unique study abroad adventure, they are shepherding up to thousands of students through the same adventure, depending on the size of your school and percent of students who go abroad.

So, take responsibility to make use of any assistance your study abroad office provides, and take responsibility for your own experience by using any and all resources available to you, whether they come through your university's support systems or not. The quality of your preparation — and thereby the quality of your experience — is ultimately up to you.

ACADEMIC PROGRESS

Unless your study abroad office has fully integrated academic advising with your school's academic departments or academic advising center, you may need to have additional conversations with your academic advisor in the semesters leading up to your study abroad experience. Some majors with lock-step curricula, like engineering, nursing, pre-med, and teacher education, make it more difficult to work in a full semester of studying abroad unless you're willing to spend additional semesters on the home campus in order to graduate.

If graduating "on time" is important to you for any reason, start investigating early which programs consistently offer courses that fit in with your field of study and will allow you to continue making progress toward graduation. Alternatively, if courses in your major are not typically available in the programs that interest you, and you can schedule courses in your major(s) and/or minor(s) with more flexibility, you may be able to postpone enough common curriculum (core) classes so that your session abroad is used to cover some of your more basic requirements toward graduation.

FINANCIAL AID

Again, your study abroad office may have integrated your financial aid considerations into its process, particularly for in-house aid. However, if you have scholarships or other financial assistance that originates from outside your institution, it's a good idea to contact whoever disburses those funds to find out if they are still available to you while studying abroad.

Likewise, if your parents, grandparents, or great aunt Velma are the source of any regular funds that support your tuition payments or fund your daily coffee habit, definitely have a conversation with them about your intention to study abroad. While they may already be supportive, it's important that you all agree on how their money will be used during your time abroad. Explain to them why you want to study abroad, what you hope to gain from the experience, and why it is important to you. Having these conversations up front will help you to know if you're on the same page, and will also give them a chance to bring up any concerns they may have. This will avoid that awkward moment where great aunt Velma sees a photo of you on Facebook with a beer in your hand and decides to stop sending the monthly checks!

Finally, check with your financial aid office, study abroad office, and/ or the university or organization managing your program for any scholarships newly available to you while studying abroad. Though not standard, there are funds designated specifically to encourage and support students with certain majors, life circumstances, or demographic characteristics to study abroad.

INTERNSHIPS, ASSISTANTSHIPS, JOBS, HOUSING

While you're abroad, the rest of the world keeps spinning. The processes that happen each year will still happen in your absence, and if you want to be a part of them, it'll take a little extra work to do that from abroad. I'm referring to endeavors such as applying for jobs or internships, applying for leadership positions on campus (like RA or student government), and applying for and securing housing (especially if you live on campus, where you have to re-commit to your housing each semester or year).

Many of these processes take place in the spring, and you'll be more likely to need help with them if you're studying abroad in the spring. If you're interested in applying for a leadership position, be sure to check with the appropriate office before you leave to find out how the process works for students abroad. And then, while you are abroad, continue to check that office's website, Twitter, Instagram, etc. so you are aware of deadlines and requirements. Even if they tell you "We'll put you on the list and send you the information when it's time," remember that you could be out-of-sight, out-of-mind. So, don't rely on someone else's memory and follow-through if what's at stake is really important to you.

If you are employed, on or off campus, talk to your employer about how your studying abroad will affect your job. Will they replace you in the interim and hold the job for you? Will you have to re-apply and compete with new applicants? Will you pick up with the same wage and standing you're leaving with? If you're not employed but would like to be upon your return, get in touch with prospective employers early — even before you leave if possible. Let them know that you'll be studying abroad, and when you return, be able to articulate how your study abroad experience has made you an even better potential employee.

HOME MATTERS

Take stock of all the significant things you own (furniture, car), owe (monthly bills), or are responsible for (pets, leadership positions). Each of these will likely need some sort of attention from you before and after your session, semester, or year abroad, and possibly also during your months abroad. Only you can know every item that falls into this category, but here are some questions to help you generate your own list:

- Do you have subscriptions (paper, physical good, or digital) that can be suspended, or canceled with a refund?
- Do you have other monthly payments (cell phone, paid digital accounts like Spotify, school loans, car payment) for which you should make arrangements?
- Do you have a housing commitment that requires attention (an apartment or room to sublet, on-campus housing spot to be given up)?
- Where will your mail go in your absence?
- Are there relatives who are elderly or sick and whom you might want to be sure to spend time with before you depart?
- Do you have recurring appointments with medical or other professionals that should be postponed?
- If you'll be out of the country when a tax deadline passes, how will you file your income tax return?

One way to track down all of these responsibilities is to be mindful of everything you do in this category for a month. Each time you pay a bill, receive a magazine, or visit the chiropractor, write it down, and at the end of the month, you'll have a pretty thorough list of everything you'll want to address before your departure.

WHAT TO PACK

How you pack and what you pack depends a great deal on what type of program you'll be attending, when you're going and how long you'll stay, and where you're studying. You can imagine that the contents of the bags packed by a student going on an applied marine biology semester in the Mediterranean would contrast dramatically with those packed by a student spending winter term in Stockholm.

If you're studying abroad for one semester or less than a full semester, you should be able to bring everything you need in one large suitcase plus one carry-on. If you're staying abroad for an entire year, you might need two suitcases (though I have seen a student successfully pack for a full academic year — nine months — in one camping backpack that was carry-on compliant! His actual carry-on was his guitar...). You'll probably be traveling within Europe often on the weekends or holidays, so you'll want a camping backpack or small suitcase that you can use for shorter weekend trips. You'll probably also want a school-sized backpack to carry your books and supplies to and from school each day; this can double as a daypack for hikes or day trips.

There are at least two good configurations in which you can have the most useful number of bags and still travel as lightly as possible. If you already own a good bag for weekend travel (a small rolling bag, duffel bag, or camping backpack) and a lightweight school-sized backpack, then I'd encourage you to bring those. Train travel can be rough on your luggage, and low-cost airline travel even more so. If you can bring old or used bags rather than brand new ones, do it. In this case, send your large suitcase as checked luggage, and pack your school backpack inside your rolling bag/duffel/camping backpack, which you'll take as your carry-on.

If you don't already own enough luggage, I would encourage you to try eBay or your local Goodwill before spending money on brand new luggage. Again, during your travels, it will be in others' hands, and it's likely to be treated roughly. Save your money to fund experiences while you're abroad.

If you really want to buy new luggage, I'd advise a combination backpack — a camping-sized backpack that has an attached small daypack that can zip off to become a separate bag. This gives you both the weekend travel bag and the school backpack, with a distinct advantage. When you return to the U.S., you can zip the daypack on to the camping backpack and check it as one piece of luggage. This means that purchases you've made while abroad have some extra space to ride home in. If you don't acquire another bag to use as your new carry-on sometime during your months abroad, you can use a shopping bag or buy a light fabric tote at any local grocery store for less than the equivalent of $5.

Perhaps just as important as what to bring in your suitcase is what not to bring. Remember that your living space will likely be smaller than a similar space in the U.S. would have been, you'll likely be traveling a lot, sharing space with others, and you'll acquire things along the way that you'll want to bring back with you.

So, especially if you're a classic over-packer, my advice would be to pack your bag and then remove half of everything you packed. Except underwear. Bring twice as much underwear as you think you need. Seriously. The number of pairs of underwear you have is directly correlated to how often you have to do laundry, and doing laundry is both expensive and time-consuming.

You can find so many opinions online about what to pack and how to squeeze it all into the tiniest suitcase possible. My packing list is just like everyone else's: it may work for you and it may not. The bottom line is that **you** know best which things you really need in order to feel comfortable and safe, and which things you can live without.

That said, here is my packing list, including what not to bring:

In your carry-on or on your person

- Passport and other ID (student ID, ISIC card, driver's license)
- Any official documents required from your host country's consulate, your program, etc.
- Wallet or purse with debit and credit cards
- Local currency
- Laptop, tablet, and/or cell phone, with charging cables and a converter
- Camera
- One change of clothes (in case of lost/delayed luggage)
- Essential toiletries in sizes that will clear security (in case of lost/delayed luggage)
- Copies of passport and other ID
- Prescriptions for the entire length of your stay (if possible — see chapter 8 for more detailed information)
- Water bottle with filter (as needed)

In your checked bag

- Compass
- Converters/adapters
- Cheap wristwatch with alarm (especially if you will not have a cell phone, but useful regardless)
- More copies of passport and other ID
- Sleep aids (earplugs, mask, medicine)
- Traveler's scarf, sleep sack, or light blanket
- Travel pillow
- Quick-dry travel towel
- Small flashlight or pen light

- Clothing (lightweight, coordinating, layerable)
- Shoes (as versatile as possible for walking, exercise, hiking)
- Cheap flip flops for shower shoes, walking around inside hostels
- Rain-proof windbreaker
- Jacket/coat as needed for your destination
- Gloves, scarves, hats as needed
- Sleepwear
- Swimwear
- Toiletries (2-week supply should suffice)
- Over-the-counter medications (pain relief, anti-motion sickness, allergy, cold medicine)
- Small power strip

What not to bring

- Hair dryer
- Valuables or irreplaceable items
- Too much of any one thing (except underwear!)
- Printed books (with some exceptions as noted)

Pro Tip: After you've packed your bag(s), take photos of their contents, and then take additional photos of the bags themselves after they are closed and ready to be checked. If your bag is lost, having a photo of it may help if you're reporting it lost in a language you don't understand. And if it stays lost, you'll have a good idea of what was in it and what the contents were worth, so that you can make a claim to your airline or insurance.

And finally, before you depart on this great adventure, make sure you have the basic skills needed to survive the streets of Europe, or wherever your studies abroad take you. The next chapter will walk you through what you need to know and how to learn it.

CHAPTER 3

Essential Skills

If you've lived in several different places, or lived in a big city you navigated on your own, you might be pretty well prepared to "hit the ground running" in your destination abroad. But if you're

You'll never plow a field by turning it over in your mind.
-Irish proverb

like the majority of American students, you probably grew up living outside a walkable downtown, traveling mostly by private car, and maybe even living in only one home or one town for your entire life. If that's the case, there are some essential skills you may not have needed so far, and developing even a beginner's level competency in those skills can help you feel more confident and comfortable in your new home abroad.

This chapter will help you assess and improve your skill sets related to map reading, navigating, using public transportation, and understanding the language and currency in your destination.

READING MAPS AND NAVIGATING

You might have learned your hometown well enough over your adolescent years that you didn't need a map or directions at all. If you've traveled some, you may have relied on GPS when you needed directions. And while GPS may be available to you in Europe, there will be times when you don't have a signal, or the battery runs out, or you just want a wider perspective on where you're going than is available on the GPS. Knowing how to read a map and navigate from point A to point B is one of the most fundamental skills you'll rely on while abroad. Whether it's in your home-base abroad, or while traveling to other places from that home-base, your ability to explore freely and enthusiastically will be bolstered by the knowledge that you can always find your way with a map.

If you already feel confident in your ability to read a map, then you can skip this section and move on. If you've rarely or never navigated on your own, without GPS, I recommend taking stock of and developing your navigational skills before departure.

THERE ARE A FEW BASIC COMPONENTS TO READING A MAP SUCCESSFULLY:

1. *Understand the cardinal directions* (north, south, east, west) and their relationship to each other. Bonus points if you can also read a compass and/or understand how to use the sun's position to help you estimate which direction is which, if you have no compass. This is foundational to finding your way around, because you can know you're heading in the right direction without actually knowing which specific street you're on.

It's also important to your overview understanding of a place. In Barcelona, the coastline runs northeast-southwest, and the city is north and west of the sea. So if you know that, and you're walking directly toward the sea, you know that you're walking in a southeasterly direction without looking at the map or compass.

2. *Know where you are* on the map, and which direction you're facing. This may seem obvious, but it's pretty difficult to navigate if you don't accurately identify your starting point. If you're staying at a hotel, hostel, or other staffed accommodation, ask the staff to mark your location on the map, including which side of the street you're on.

If you can't determine which direction you're facing, walk a block to see the name of the next cross street, and check that against your map so you'll know which direction you walked.

3. *Know where you want to go*. A self-explanatory but essential step. Be sure that your destination is actually on the map you're using.

4. *Be able to plot a route* between where you are and where you're headed. Pay attention to the quality of the streets on your route (pedestrian vs. traffic/public transit route, small back alley vs. wide shopping avenue), noting any options that may make the route easier or more difficult. Note, too, when you might be able to see something additional on your way to your destination, like walking through a park instead of only on streets, or going one or two blocks out of your way to pass by a well-known monument or famous café.

You might find it useful to plot a couple of possible routes, so that you have options if there are real-life obstacles not shown on the map (like a parade or demonstration, temporary road closure, construction).

5. *Understand and pay attention to the map's legend and scale*. Symbols can help you navigate, but so can more subtle indicators, like the color or thickness of lines, or the shading or pattern of certain areas. For example, many maps will indicate pedestrian-only areas with a cobblestone pattern on those streets. A pedestrian area, elevated tramway, or parking lot can be just as useful a landmark as a monument or museum.

A few more tips:

- Some tourist maps have images of monuments and other major attractions printed on them to help with quick recognition.

However, often these images are oriented so that the front of the monument is facing you (the map reader), regardless of the perspective of the map. When you're using this type of map to navigate, don't assume that you can trust the orientation of the monument to the map itself.

- Some tourist maps are not drawn to a consistent scale. For example, the walkable part of the city center is shown at a 1:25,000 scale, but at some border (which may or may not be obvious), the scale changes to 1:100,000 so that the map can include attractions in the outskirts or suburbs of the city. If you don't realize this change of scale, it might look like you could walk to a particular destination in half an hour, when in fact it might take more like two and a half hours (and involve roads not suited to pedestrians).

- If you don't have a strong innate sense of direction and need more help with map reading, search "how to read a map" online. There are lots of free resources available for map-readers of all levels.

- More than other kinds of maps, tourist maps might prioritize matching the shape of a particular district to the shape of the paper it's printed on over keeping north at the top of the map. Especially on smaller maps depicting just one district of a city, be sure to check the compass rose to confirm the map's orientation.

- Most free tourist maps are paid for at least in part with advertising dollars. When you see restaurants or other businesses on the map, remember that they are there because they paid to be there. Their presence on the map doesn't indicate an endorsement, or say anything (positive or negative) about their quality or service.

- While digital maps are usually very accurate and often readily accessible, paper maps give you a much broader view of the place you're navigating. You can write on them to mark routes, safely pull them out in the rain, and they're functional even if the wifi isn't working! If maps are available for free at your hotel or the local tourist office, consider getting one for each day of your trip and plotting each day's plan on its own map.

- Evaluate your navigational skills before you leave home! You'll find a map-reading exercise in the workbook for some ideas on how to put yourself to the test.

USING PUBLIC TRANSPORTATION

Depending on where you've lived, you might already have a good understanding of how to use public transport. If so, there's no need for you to continue with this section. If you haven't used public transport at all, or haven't used it on your own, this section will help prepare you for understanding and using public transportation to find your way around cities where public transportation is available.

Many European cities have multiple, integrated modes of public transport. In the largest cities, a train system (called tube or metro or subway depending on the city) often covers longer distances with less frequent stops, while buses supplement the coverage with more local service and more frequent stops. In many cases, one ticket will cover a single ride in the system, whether you are taking the train or bus or a combination of both.

Reading public transport maps will rely on your general map-reading skills, plus some additional attention to detail. A map of the transport system may stand alone, or may be overlaid on a map of the city. Often the standalone maps are stylized, meaning they do not depict the actual path of the train tracks, but the relative path. A stylized map might show as a straight horizontal line what, on a map, would look more like an upward-trending zigzag. So, if you're using a combination of public transportation and walking to reach your destination, it's important to combine information from different sources, so that you see where your desired bus or train stop is in relation to other known locations in the city.

Most transit maps will identify each "line" of service by a number, name, color, or some combination of the three. Where lines cross, you can get off one train and get on another going in a different direction. This is typically called a "transfer," and the stations where this can happen are called transfer stations. So, if you realize you're on the wrong train or bus and need to get off at the upcoming stop, you'll want to ask, "Is this a transfer station?" If it's not, all you can do from there is walk, or get back on the same train or bus later (going in the same or the opposite direction). If you want to make a turn in your route, you'll need a transfer station.

The direction of a line is most often identified by the name of the last station on the line, the one where the train or bus stops and turns around to repeat the route in the opposite direction. That last station is called the "end line." Sometimes, the direction instead is identified with a cardinal point, e.g. "westbound." In this case it's especially critical to know how the metro map relates to the map of the city. In the workbook, you'll find a few examples demonstrating how to read the London tube map.

If you're taking a bus or train, it's also good to understand how to read the timetable. You'll likely be at a bus stop/train station platform and need to know that you're getting on the right bus/train, that it's going in the right direction, when the next bus/train should arrive, and when you should get off. Some examples to help you recognize how to read timetables can be found in the workbook.

Ticket Validity

When using public transportation in any city, you'll need to know how to buy a ticket, how to be sure the ticket is valid, and what type or length of ride(s) the ticket supports.

Most systems have different types of tickets that offer lower fares to those who use the system the most. The cost of a single-ride ticket is usually higher than the cost of a single ride purchased as part of a ticket package, day pass, multi-day pass, or monthly pass. Discounts may also be available for students, so if you'll be riding public transit regularly in your home-base abroad, check to see if you can get a monthly pass at a student price (in Europe, this perk is often reserved for students who are EU citizens, but it's worth asking).

If you're traveling with a single-use paper ticket, you almost always have to validate the ticket (by having it timestamped in a machine either on board or at the stop) in order for it to be valid. Why? Paper tickets are typically blank, valid for any single ride. So, if you didn't have to validate it, people could just ride around with the same ticket for their whole lives... which would not provide enough revenue for the system to continue running. (Exception: in many northern European countries, the only way to purchase a single ticket is from the driver as you board, in which case you need no further validation.)

What's more, most systems have a *temporal and directional* limit to the validity of a ticket. For example, the ticket might be valid for up to 90 minutes from the timestamp, which would allow you to make most trips possible within the system on one fare. However, most tickets are also only valid in one direction, regardless of time. In other words, you can't get on a bus, ride for five minutes, run a quick errand, and then use the same ticket to get back on the bus and return in the direction from which you came, even if you're able to complete all of that within the stated time limit for a fare. Rules vary, so check the documentation on the ticket or available at the point of purchase of the ticket, but don't assume and you'll be more likely to have a peaceful ride.

Remember that many of the other riders on the bus are locals, daily users who have a pass of some kind and therefore do not need to validate a one-off ticket. Don't let this fool you into thinking no one is buying tickets! If controllers conduct a random check of the passengers (which happens more than you might imagine), anyone who cannot produce a valid ticket will be fined and can be subject to other penalties. Riding without a ticket is theft; it's not worth the risk!

UNDERSTANDING THE LANGUAGE

Understanding the local language — or even becoming fluent — may be an important part of your goals for studying abroad. On the other hand, you may be looking for international experience and to expand your boundaries, but not want to invest a lot of time learning a language that you may never use after your time abroad ends.

As a practical matter and as a way of showing respect for the places you visit and their people, you should have at least a minimum vocabulary in the local language. This is true for your home-base abroad and for any other destination, even if you're only visiting for a weekend.

Free resources to help you with basic language learning are widely available online and as apps. There are some common words that are always recommended to assist you in communicating politely with locals, like

Hello | Goodbye | Please | Thank you | Nice to meet you. | Where is the toilet? | May I have the check? | How much does this cost?

But there is another set of functional vocabulary that can make a major difference in the quality of your experience, especially when you're visiting a third-language location for just a few days. These are words like train | ticket | price | fare | exit | help | platform | bus stop | schedule | departure | arrival | left | right | straight ahead | up | down | flight | gate | security

You don't need to memorize these words in every language! Write down the ones I've suggested and any others you can think of, and continue to build the list as you travel and realize which words are most useful to you. As you prepare to travel to a new destination, look up all of the words on your list in the target language, and write them on an index card, map, or other easily accessible place so that you can pull them out quickly and use them when you need them.

Using the local language, even badly, will usually go a long way with the local people. If they see that you're trying, they'll appreciate that and be more willing to help you.

CONVERTING CURRENCY

We'll cover many other money-related topics in a later chapter, but converting currency accurately is one of those basic skills that will make your experience so much smoother. Once you've lived in a Euro-zone country for a while you'll get used to the slight difference between the Euro and the dollar, but it's smart to pay attention to changes in the currencies' value.

If, for example, you need to withdraw money from an ATM, and the Euro has been getting stronger day by day (that is, it takes more dollars to buy the same number of Euros as the days pass), then you should go ahead and withdraw your money as soon as possible. On the other hand, if the Euro is getting weaker day by day (so, it takes fewer dollars to buy the same number of Euros as the days pass), then you might wait to withdraw your money.

Other currencies can be more complicated to convert. For example, if you travel to Budapest, you'll need Hungarian forints to purchase anything locally. One forint, at this writing, is about .0035 dollars, or .0032 Euros, and unless you're a mental math whiz, those numbers probably mean you'll either have to use a calculator or just guess at how much you're spending and hope you don't break the bank. If you can come up with a good, simple equation for tricky conversions — even if it's just a rough estimate — it'll be easier to keep track of how much you're spending overall and how much you're paying for individual meals, souvenirs, and the like.

Examples

$1 = 286 HUF and

€1 = 316 HUF

Doing the conversion in your head with numbers like 286 and 316 would take a long time. So, you want to simplify the number to an estimate.

286 is closer to 300 than to 250, but if you round up to 300, then you're pretending that one dollar will buy you 300 HUF, when in fact it will only buy you 286. So, I prefer to round down to 250, and just keep in mind that the actual cost for everything is really a little less than the estimate I'm calculating.

If you pretend that $1 = 250 HUF, then

$10 = 2500 HUF

$20 = 5000 HUF

$100 = 25000 HUF

Find a pattern in these numbers that you can recognize and remember. For me, it's "drop three zeros from the HUF number and multiply by four." So, if I see a price of 50,000 HUF, I can easily know that's about $200. (If you do the math: 50,000/286 = $174.83, so I think I'm spending "a little less than $200" and in fact, it's about $175. That's close enough for me, and the difference covers the little things I sometimes I forget I'm spending on, like snacks, or things I forget to factor in, like tips.)

One more example. If you've got a good understanding of how much a Euro is worth (because you've been living in a Euro-zone country for a while, perhaps), then you might be able to think in Euros instead of dollars. Remember, the Euro will buy you 316 HUF.

So if you pretend that €1 = 300 HUF, then

€5 = 1500 HUF

€10 = 3000 HUF

€100 = 30000 HUF

Again, find a pattern in these numbers that you can recognize and remember. The most obvious one to me here is "drop two zeros and divide by three." So, using the same check as above, something with a 50,000 HUF price tag would cost about €166. The real conversion is 50,000/316 = €158.23, which again, is close enough for me.

With all of the other decisions you have to make and situations you have to consider, learning how to convert currency in your head may seem like a minuscule detail not worth prioritizing. However, knowing how much you're paying isn't just a matter of avoiding overpriced food or souvenirs. If you take a taxi and the driver tells you how much you owe on arrival, being able to convert currency quickly can be the difference between paying a fair price and getting overcharged. Or, if you're negotiating with a vendor on the price of an item, you'll be able to know your limits and buy or choose not to buy according to the price that is acceptable to you. There are dozens of other examples like this, but in general, feeling confident in your ability to understand how much something costs will help you navigate a new place with ease.

If you can get a good grasp on reading maps, navigating, using public transportation, and converting currency before you depart, you'll begin your term abroad with many of the basic skills you need to get through the day. And, you'll feel a lot more confident from day one.

CHAPTER 4

On Health and Wellness

Maintaining good health while traveling can be a challenge for anyone. Changing time zones, sleeping in unfamiliar quarters, and exposure to different bacteria are just a few factors

Take care of your body. It's the only place you have to live.
-Jim Rohn

that can influence your health and overall feeling of well-being. When you're going on vacation, a health incident can make you feel like you've wasted your time and money, and you're just counting the days until you can get home to your doctor (or at least your familiar foods/water/bed). But when you're spending a semester or year abroad, health challenges can go from minor to major to life-threatening, so it's especially critical to pay attention to your health and wellness, know what resources are available to you, and address problems quickly. A stomach bug from eating unfamiliar foods can compromise your immune system enough to knock you out for a week or two if you don't give your body the time and rest it needs to heal. I've seen illnesses as simple as ear infections put a damper on a student's entire semester abroad, because they just couldn't ever get well, and constantly feeling unwell led to sadness, lost opportunity, and even depression.

That said, there's a long list of things you can do to support your health and well-being while abroad!

In this chapter, I'll help you identify some health-related areas which may cause difficulty or need your attention while you're abroad, and give you some tips to manage your health, in both preventive and reactive ways.

STAY HYDRATED

In many parts of the world, water is neither a given nor complimentary addition to your meal. For some, having to pay for water combined with being afraid to drink tap water can result in a chronic state of dehydration for the course of their stay! If you're worried about the tap water, do some research by talking to other travelers or reading online. If you decide you won't drink tap water, or you have a bad reaction, find a grocery store. There you can buy large bottles of water much more cheaply than single-serving bottles in a restaurant or cafe. If you suspect this will be a problem for you ahead of time, it might be worth investing in a bottle with a good filter and taking it with you. However you manage it, be sure you're getting enough water to keep your baseline health strong.

BE MINDFUL OF WHAT YOU EAT

If differences in water quality can cause problems, then differences in recipes, kitchens, sanitary practices, and available ingredients can practically create an obstacle course for anyone interested in sampling local cuisine and wanting to remain healthy in the process. Depending on where you travel, regulation of restaurants, food carts, coffee shops, and other food vendors may vary wildly from what you're accustomed to at home. One way to increase your chances of eating healthy food that was prepared properly — and that won't make you sick — is to eat where the locals eat. I say *increase* your chances because you have to remember that the locals are used to the ingredients and the preparation style of the food in their own country. I also don't want to scare you or warn you off from trying as many new foods, and especially local specialties, as appeal to you. Many, many people travel frequently and all over the world and never experience food-related illness. **Please don't let the fear of becoming ill prevent you from enjoying the wonders of any cuisine that's new to you!**

At the same time, you can take some precautions to ensure that you have the best chance of staying healthy while abroad, and know what to do if you react to something you eat.

Allergies: If you have life-threatening or serious allergic reactions to known ingredients, it is critical that you know how to communicate what you are allergic to, and what medical treatment you need if you are exposed to the allergen. Make a small card to keep in your wallet that has the English name of your allergen(s), and image if appropriate and recognizable, and the translation for that allergen in any languages you think you'll need during the course of your travels. You'll find an example, and a template to help you create your own, in the workbook.

Before departure, it's a good idea to have your doctor write specific instructions on how to treat you during an allergic reaction. Any medicines referenced in these instructions should be described by their generic names (or chemical formula), and not by a brand name, since brand names vary from market to market. Keep a copy of this with you all the time – a digital copy in your phone, a paper copy in your wallet, or both.

If you have non-life-threatening but uncomfortable and avoidable reactions to certain foods, such as a dairy intolerance, it's a good idea to bring with you any over-the-counter medication *that you know works for you* in preventing or relieving symptoms. While you may be able to find similar medications abroad, slight variations in concentration or ingredients may mean they don't work as effectively for you. And, let's be honest, the first time you pass an Italian gelateria, you don't want to go looking for a pharmacy. You just want the gelato.

Preferences: Depending on where you'll be traveling, and how important your preferences are to you, it can be a good idea to present your preferences as allergies. If you are vegetarian or vegan, or you avoid certain foods for religious reasons or because of a strong moral stance, you'll need to take the cultural temperature to determine whether your preferences will be honored if presented as preferences, or if you need to give them more weight by presenting them as allergies. For example, in cultures where veganism is less common, you might be told a dish that uses beef stock as the base for its sauce is vegan, because there's no animal flesh in the dish. I don't believe this comes from a malicious desire to force vegans to consume animal products, but rather a different interpretation of *vegan*. In my early years in Italy, at group meals, those who ordered vegetarian dishes would often be served fish. At that time, to some people, "I don't eat meat" meant "I don't eat beef, pork, or chicken." (By 2015, several vegan cafés had opened in Florence, and were thriving.) So it's important to understand the cultural perspective of your location in general, and to learn to be very specific when making requests in any restaurant or café.

IMPORTANT: Please, please do not use your preferences as a way to stay in your culinary comfort zone and avoid ever experiencing the true flavors of your host country's cuisine. If you go to a restaurant and a dish features sage, and you don't like sage, don't ask if they can substitute a different herb in the dish. The dish is made with sage for a reason. Just choose another entrée. Or, realize that it's possible that you will experience sage in a whole new way by trying it in this dish. And maybe you'll like it after all!

ALCOHOL

There's really a lot to say about consumption of alcohol while abroad. Unfortunately, the majority of what I want to share with you about alcohol consumption is found in the chapter on safety and security. Here, I'd just like to talk about alcohol from a health and wellness perspective. But it's certainly essential that you read and retain the section on alcohol and safety.

When you imagine a semester abroad, you probably have visions of dining al fresco, drinking, eating, and chatting with your new international friends. Or of nightly dinner with your local hosts, where even the young kids are served a watered-down glass of wine, because it's just no big deal in their culture. It's a component of the meal that is given. Or maybe your image is of a pub or beer garden, where you meet and mix with locals in an authentic cultural and social experience.

You might also imagine hanging out with new American friends — and new local friends — at a club, staying out as late as you want, being totally in control of your time and experience. All of these scenarios are possible, even likely. If you want to define your experience abroad, rather than letting one or two choices define that experience for you, pay close attention to how your attitudes and actions involving alcohol fit – or do not fit — into the cultural and social landscape.

You've probably already heard a lot about the differences in norms of alcohol consumption in the U.S. and other countries.

You may have heard the other countries have no minimum legal drinking age (true, but for very few countries; 70% of the world's countries have a minimum legal drinking age between 16 and 19). Underage drinking is not an American phenomenon. Teenagers in other countries engage in underage drinking as well. The difference is whether you're experimenting at 15 while living in the structured environment of home or at 19, living on your own. Whether you live in a culture that sees alcohol as a typical component of any meal, or in a culture in which **the age at which young people experiment most heavily with alcohol consumption and at which they leave home to live on their own for the first time tragically coincide.** Having worked, lived, and traveled throughout Europe with American college students abroad for almost a decade, I can confidently say that the local response to students' alcohol-related behaviors is most often one of disgust and disdain. But I digress. I'm leaning into a conversation better suited for another chapter (and I'll pick this up again there).

What I really want to say here is this: like food and water, alcoholic beverages may not be consistent with your expectations. They may be stronger, more concentrated, or more diverse in their ingredients than what your body is used to. Your style of consuming alcoholic beverages may affect your health and wellness because it identifies you immediately as a foreigner or tourist. And if you do overconsume, the response from local medical professionals may vary dramatically from the kind of response you'd get at home. Sympathy can be quite low for foreign students who drink so much that they end up in the hospital, using public resources, for something that's considered a juvenile and avoidable problem.

The bottom line? Take it slow, take it easy, and remember this may be your only chance to live abroad. *Revel in that opportunity.* You have a whole lifetime to drink wine.

FITNESS

It can be difficult to maintain a fitness routine while abroad, especially if you're used to living on campus where state-of-the-art fitness facilities are available to you 24/7. In addition to the feeling that you have a limited time to see and do all the things that appeal to you, you've also got a limited time to try countless new foods and drinks, not to mention meeting new people, going to class, and actually studying! How can you fit in a fitness routine, especially if there's no gym or other facility to support you? Should you? Is it even important?

Or should you just give yourself a "semester off" and worry about it when you get home?

The answer will be different for everyone. Depending on your schedule and circumstances, it may just be too difficult to squeeze in workouts and still make the most of your experience abroad. However, I would encourage you to find whatever ways you can to maintain your body's health – even if that means stretching in your room each night, or choosing to walk sometimes when you could have taken the bus. Maintaining good physical health provides a strong foundation for your emotional well-being, your mental health, and your body's ability to fight off infection or heal from injury.

If you are involved in organized sports, or have any kind of consistent fitness routine, and your body is used to regular physical exertion, you may be affected even more negatively in an environment that doesn't support regular workouts. If you are not currently doing much physical activity, you may find it very taxing to keep up with the pace of living abroad. Whichever end of the spectrum you're on, prepare to support your health while abroad by finding some simple exercises you can start now and continue while abroad without the need for special equipment or a lot of space.

In my nine years in Florence, I saw a pattern emerge that I can't explain scientifically, but that I want to share with you nonetheless. My students, like most other American students in Italy, were eating lots of great Italian food, drinking beautiful Italian wine, working out (on average) much less than they had at home, and walking everywhere. Walking was their primary mode of transportation — for academic purposes, for local personal purposes, and when they traveled outside of Italy.

And it's a great way to get around. For one thing, it's free. But it also slows you down, and lets you experience the world around you in a much more intimate way than from the inside of a bus or subway car. The pattern I saw unfolded in this way: in the first several weeks abroad, students ate and drank much more than their typical caloric intake. They didn't get into a fitness routine from day one. A few weeks into the semester, the women would start to complain that their clothes were getting a little tight, so they would make a conscious effort not to overeat. The men did not seem to have the same problem. In fact, many of the men actually noticed that despite eating and drinking more, they were losing weight. After years of observing this phenomenon, and dozens if not hundreds of conversations with students about it, I have drawn the (again, completely unscientific) conclusion that for many women, walking, no matter how much of it they do, just does not create enough aerobic activity to contribute to maintaining a healthy weight. Meanwhile, the men lost weight even while eating more and exercising less. In many cases, their only physical activity was walking, and still they lost weight. It may not work this way for you, but I saw the pattern consistently enough that it seems important to mention. You cannot know now if your experience will follow this pattern or not. What you can do, if you already have a fitness routine, is find ways to maintain it (at least to some degree) while abroad, and not rely on walking as your only form of physical activity.

BUMPS IN THE ROAD

Sometimes being abroad can alert you to health-related issues you were previously unaware of, or create circumstances, new to you, in which your health is compromised.

Motion sickness. Many times, I saw students who had never before suffered from motion sickness miserably trapped on a multi-hour bus or boat ride feeling faint, nauseous, and even vomiting (not that fun on a 50-passenger coach). Even if you feel 100% immune to motion sickness, it will cost you almost nothing to bring a small bottle of Dramamine (or your choice of anti-motion-sickness meds) along, just in case. Yes, the same type of medication may be available in your destination, but it will likely cost more, and by the time you know you need it, it might be too late to find a pharmacy.

Bedbugs. Bedbugs are now a worldwide, pervasive problem. No hotel, hostel, or home is immune; their presence is no longer an indication of poor sanitary conditions, so you can't be sure to avoid them just by choosing expensive lodging. They are extremely difficult to get rid of, and their bites cause itching, inflammation, and sometimes scarring. The best possible bedbug solution is not to be exposed to them in the first place!

How do you avoid them? When you check in to a hostel or hotel room, don't drop your luggage on the bed first thing! Leave it in the bathroom or on another tiled (or at least not carpeted) surface, far from the bed. Then, check the bed by lifting the mattress and examining the underside, especially the grooves in the bed frame and the underside of the sheets. Look for spots of blood, bug carcasses, or small spots of excrement. You most likely will not see bugs, since they hide from light and only move around in the dark. When born, bedbugs are translucent and about the size of a poppy seed. Adults are reddish-brown and no larger than an apple seed. If you see evidence of bedbugs, ask to be moved to a different room before moving any of your belongings in proximity of the bed or carpets. Even if you avoid them in your hotel, bedbugs can be transferred from one piece of luggage to another, so after you travel, inspect your luggage before bringing it into your permanent residence. If you have a hard-sided bag, you only need to examine the cloth parts (zippers, maybe luggage tag). If your bag is soft, you should examine the whole thing, preferably in sunlight, to check for bugs or larvae. If the unthinkable happens, and you bring bedbugs back into your own home, consult a professional as soon as possible. The longer they are there, the harder they are to get rid of. You can find lots more info online about bedbugs, from prevention to cure.

Temperature regulation. Heating and cooling practices in the U.S. tend to favor comfort over cost savings or reducing environmental impact. In other parts of the world, the cost of heating and cooling can be significantly higher, the awareness of environmental impact deeper, and the American tendency to seal up the building and keep the outside outside may be viewed as odd, at best. If you're traveling in cold months, this may mean wearing more clothes inside than is your habit, and needing flannel pajamas, scarves, slippers, hats, mittens, etc. that you might not need at home (depending on where you live). In warm months, it may mean sleeping with the windows open, having windows without screens, not having air conditioning, or air conditioning for the bedroom only. It may mean buying a fan at a local discount store. If you're one of those people whom bugs just love to bite, consider whether you might benefit from a bug-repelling sleep sack and/or clothing, and an anti-itch cream that you know works best for you. In addition to making you more comfortable in waking hours, having the right tools can also help you get more and better sleep.

Speaking of sleep. You'll be sleeping in unfamiliar beds, most likely in conditions you can't fully understand until you get to your destination. Sleep is essential to your health, so be prepared to make adjustments as necessary to be sure you're able to get enough quality sleep. If you need significant darkness or silence to sleep, bring an eyemask or earplugs. (If you plan to travel from your home-base destination, you'll probably be staying in hostels, sharing space with people you don't know, which makes those even more useful.) If you know you tend to get cold at night, bring a thin but warm scarf that can double as an extra layer between you and the sheets. If you're a worrier, think ahead of time about how you'll store your valuables when you're sharing a room with strangers. Many hostels have lockers, but you might have to provide the lock yourself. In addition, there's usually the option of leaving your valuables checked at the front desk. A travel pillow can also boost your sleep potential, both while in transit and if you end up with ho(s)tel-provided pillows that don't suit you.

Prescriptions. Check the legality of any prescription drugs you use before you travel. Some medications that are legal in the U.S. are not legal in other countries. If you take a medication that falls in this category, it's vital to talk to your doctor long before you leave; if you need to switch to a legal alternative, you'll want to do that months ahead of time so you're sure the new medication works for you and that you've gotten past any withdrawal or switching discomfort before you travel. If at all possible, take the prescriptions you'll need for your entire time abroad, and be sure they are in their original prescription bottles with your name on them, so there's no question that they are yours, and that they are legal. If that means a large quantity of medicine, it's even better if you can have a formal letter from your doctor as additional evidence that you need the medication. If you'll be gone longer than your insurance will pre-approve your prescription, do your research ahead of time to figure out how and where you'll be able to fill the prescription abroad. You'll most likely need a prescription from a local doctor, as yours won't be honored out-of-country.

Pharmacists can be a great resource for non-urgent medical needs. If you're feeling under the weather, but not bad enough to require a visit to a doctor, stop by the local pharmacy. You can tell the pharmacist your symptoms, and he or she will recommend over-the-counter remedies, and tell you under what change in conditions you should go ahead and see a doctor.

Know your coverage. Most countries legally require you to have health coverage in order to live and study there. (Even if they didn't, it would still be a really, really good idea.) Whether you are studying through your home campus, another campus whose program is approved by your school, or an independent operator, health insurance is almost certainly both offered and required. Although it's not the most exciting topic in the world, please be sure you're informed about how your coverage works. If you need it, you'll be in a much better position to use it; sifting through insurance documents is the last thing you want to do when you're ill or injured and just need help.

Some Questions to Consider

- How is emergency care handled?
- Do you have to clear your visit before going to a hospital? What if you are transported by ambulance and unable to contact the insurer in advance?

- Do you have to schedule non-emergency appointments through the provider?
- How does billing work? Should you expect to pay up front and be reimbursed, or does the insurer have agreements in place to be billed directly by the health care provider?
- Will your copay increase while you're abroad? Will you have to submit receipts immediately, or can you wait until your term ends to send them to your insurance carrier?
- Is there coverage for medical evacuation, should that be needed?
- How do you access the insurer, and are they available 24 hours a day?
- Can your parent (or other representative) talk to them on your behalf?
- Is mental health care covered, and if so, under what circumstances?
- Are there exclusions for issues considered to be high risks, such as adventure sports or drug or alcohol overdose?

Finally, be sure that a parent or trusted loved one has a valid passport and is willing and able to travel to you in an emergency. Should you need to be hospitalized far away from home, you'll want to know that someone can be there with you as soon as possible.

The number of specific medical issues we could cover is infinite, and most of them will (thankfully) never be relevant to you. The most important takeaway here is not to take your health and well-being for granted, to do what you can to protect them, and to know how best to respond if you do need healthcare or support.

Finally, if you get sick or injured, don't wait it out and hope it will get better! Small problems can turn into critical ones if left untreated, and it's much easier to treat a small problem than a critical one.

CHAPTER 5

Money, Mail, Laundry, and Other Logistics

Living — or even visiting — abroad, you'll have questions on almost a daily basis. Activities that are automatic, or that you take for granted at home, will

Smooth seas do not make skillful sailors.
-African proverb

suddenly require extra knowledge. Where do I buy groceries? Why did I get a slip in the mail instead of the package I was waiting for? What's the best way to get cash? Where can I find a notebook for class that doesn't cost more than my last meal? Do I really have to go to the immigration office? I'm a student, not an immigrant! Why did my hair dryer almost start a fire, even though I was using a converter?

In this chapter, I'll try to give you some insider information — collected over years of experiencing small frustrations myself and with my students — so that the little things in life don't trip you up. In no particular order...

MONEY & PAYING FOR STUFF

Although I'd like to say that there's no reason to carry a lot of cash with you as you travel, the truth is that sometimes systems don't work the way they're supposed to, and having cash is the only way to be sure you can get to where you need to go. So, before you leave, get the equivalent of about $200 in the currency of your destination. For the purpose of this discussion, we'll talk about Euros.

Where do you get those Euros? If you know someone who's traveling to your destination and returning before you depart, you could ask them to bring some cash back for you, and you could buy it from them at a fair market rate. Otherwise, you'll need to talk to your bank and purchase the Euros there (where you'll probably pay a commission and get a rate that favors the bank). If you live in a smaller town or use a smaller bank, you may have to order the currency ahead of time, while big banks in big cities typically have common currencies on hand and available for immediate sale.

If all goes well, once you've got that initial wad of cash, you shouldn't have to deal with banks for the duration of your time abroad.

Many credit companies now offer cards with no fees for international purchases. Visa and MasterCard (note I did not say American Express or Discover) are widely accepted throughout Europe. So, if you have a no-fee credit card, you can use it most of the time, for most of your purchases. But there will still be venues that only accept local bankcards or cash.

So, you need a way to have access to cash, and the simplest road to cash is through an ATM, with your debit card. Some larger U.S. banks have agreements with or are members of global networks, and allow fee-free withdrawals from ATMs within the network. Others will reimburse you for ATM fees up to a certain dollar amount or a certain number of times per year. Look into your options (including opening a new account just for this purpose) to save as much as possible on ATM fees; they really add up, and I've seen machines with individual fees as high as €6! If you can't get to zero on ATM fees, then you'll want to budget and plan well so that you don't have to withdraw cash frequently. If you know you can get by on €200 per month in cash, then withdraw that amount once a month, put it in a safe place, and only carry with you as much as you need on any given day. Use a similar system if you have multiple credit and/or debit cards; take just one with you at a time, and leave the rest in a safe place at home to minimize your losses in case of theft.

ACADEMIC SUPPLIES

When you're packing for an entire semester or year abroad, you won't want to use precious space or weight allowance on notebooks, textbooks, or other academic supplies that can be obtained abroad. Your school or program should have information about textbooks; many programs either provide books onsite, have agreements with local bookstores, or use digital textbooks or collections of readings freely available online in place of textbooks. If none of these is true for you, and you must acquire your textbooks yourself, you can still avoid purchasing them all ahead of time and lugging them to an airport. One solution, if you know some of your fellow students, is to organize a textbook sharing system, whereby each of you buys a fraction of the books needed, so that together you have at least one of everything. However, be careful with this system; if you don't live close to the others in your group, the logistics of using the same book (that everyone needs at the same time, for the same assignments) can be daunting.

Another solution — whether you know which books you'll need ahead of time or not — is to order online and have the books shipped to your school or home address abroad. If you know which books you'll need before departure, check sites local to your destination to see if you can order the books there. Amazon.co.uk (where you can find many textbooks in English) ships to most European countries, and Amazon has separate sites for many other countries (amazon.fr, amazon.it, etc.) if you're looking for books in the native language. There are also plenty of other resources online for finding books to be shipped within the EU, for example, rather than paying for international shipping from the US and waiting for the package to clear customs. If you're taking classes with big, heavy books that can only be purchased in the U.S., another option is to pay for an additional checked bag on your flight, pack the books in a sturdy box, and send them as a checked bag. This option should be cheaper and is definitely faster than having the books shipped internationally direct from the source. If you can share the box and extra cost with someone else, even better.

For cheap and basic school supplies, find a "Euro Store" (they are sometimes also called "99 Cent" store, or, in the UK, "Poundland."). They carry a variety of products that are useful for school, including pens, paper, notebooks, folders, markers, etc., though you can't be particular about what's on the cover of your notebook (think kittens or 90's TV lore). But for the basic needs of taking notes in class and keeping yourself organized for the semester, they'll do the trick.

LAUNDRY

There are self-serve laundromats all over Europe, and you can usually either put coins directly into the machines or buy tokens from a machine inside the laundromat. A common scam, at least in Europe, is perpetrated by people looking to steal your money or wallet. They will hang out in the laundromat and act like they don't understand how to use the machines, then ask you (in the local language, which you may not understand, or in broken English, which you have to concentrate to try to understand) to help them figure out how to do their laundry. While you are distracted, helping them, an accomplice makes off with your wallet, phone, or backpack. Many of these laundromats are open late hours and are not staffed, so they can be dangerous places to hang out.

Safety tip: Don't take any valuables to the laundromat, avoid going late at night if at all possible, and avoid going alone.

In many cities, entrepreneurial types have seen the constant ebb and flow of students and tourists and created services to address your laundry needs. Look around, or ask a concierge at a small, local hotel, for any information on a laundry service. For about the same price as doing your own laundry, and without spending your precious hours at the laundromat, you can have your laundry done for you at a full-service laundromat. Sometimes full service is available as an option at the self-serve laundromats; other times, you'll find the full-service option at a dry cleaner. Typically, you drop off a bag of laundry and pick it up 24-48 hours later, washed and dried. If you find a place like this, before you discount it for being too expensive, compare it to what it really costs you to do your own laundry. Often self-serve laundromat dryers are neither well-calibrated nor well-ventilated, so it takes multiple drying cycles per load to get your clothes dry. If you have space at home to hang wet laundry, and are willing to haul wet clothes home from the laundromat, then washing and hanging to dry is probably the most economical option. But if you have to use the dryers, too, consider whether a full-service option will save you money and/or time.

CONVERTERS AND ADAPTERS

First, know the difference: a converter changes the actual amount of electricity passing from the outlet into your electrical appliance. An adapter simply receives the prongs of your power cord and then fits into the local outlet with its "local style" prongs, without modifying the strength of the electricity passing through it in any way. Some converters are also adapters; no adapters are also converters. American appliances run on 110 volts, while in Europe, they run on 220 volts. This means that if you plug in an appliance from the U.S. without a converter (or transformer, as it's called when it's built in), you're sending it twice the amount of electricity it's made to use. And it will burn up. Even with a converter, hair dryers seem to be problematic. I have seen dozens of converters burned up because they were used with American hair dryers in Florence. This is why I advise against bringing a hair dryer. If you absolutely must dry your hair, it's better to buy a small dryer at your destination than bring one that will just be trash after the first or second use.

Most expensive electronics (laptops, tablets, phones) have a power cable that already includes a transformer, in the (usually black) box or "power brick." You'll know whether yours does or not by reading the fine print on the brick. If it says "INPUT 100-240V," then you're in good shape and all you need is an adapter.

Since power outlets are fewer in Europe than in the U.S., and in many cases when you're studying abroad, you're sharing a space (and therefore, available outlets) with other students, I recommend bringing a small power strip (2-3 extra outlets + 2 USB charging ports, even better if it also has surge protection) along with your adapter. You'll be able to charge all of your devices even if there's only one wall outlet available to you.

RECEIVING MAIL & CARE PACKAGES

While you're away, your family and friends might want to send you care packages or other postal love to let you know you're missed. That's great! There's something about receiving a tangible message from a loved one that can brighten your spirit more than an email ever could. However, be sure to talk with potential senders about what they can easily send and what should be avoided, so that nothing important gets lost in the mail, or caught up in customs for so long that you don't receive it while you're abroad.

Letters will usually make their way through the postal systems just fine. Be sure that letters only contain letters — no cash, no jewelry tucked into the envelope, no gum or candy. A plain letter with adequate postage will have no problem.

Packages are another matter. First, anyone who sends a package through U.S. mail will be given a delivery estimate — typically "seven to ten days." This estimate is the number of days it takes for the U.S. Postal Service to deliver the package to the postal service in the destination country. At that point, delivery is the responsibility of another postal service, and may happen within a day (best case) or may take several weeks (or, worst case, more). The point here is that urgently-needed items should not be sent via the postal systems. Once you have received non-urgent items and have a sense of how efficient the postal system in your country is, then you'll know how reliable it is for time-sensitive deliveries.

Once again, it depends on which country you're in, but any package (regardless of contents) may be subject to an import tax that the recipient has to pay before the package is released. Sometimes no tax is levied, but if the items in the package are new and have any value to speak of, usually some tax is owed (the more the package is worth, the more is owed). So, if someone is sending you some of your old sweatpants and sweatshirts because it's colder than you thought, tell them to resist the temptation to overvalue the box's contents in hopes of making a sweet insurance claim on a lost package. What will likely happen instead is that you'll be required to pay 20-some percent of whatever they indicated the value was, just to have your old clothes.

The biggest hang-ups I've seen in package delivery were with care packages. Care packages usually contain gum, candy, food, lotions, lip balms, vitamins, protein bars, etc. — all the comforts from home, your favorite brands and flavors and homemade baked goods that just aren't available in your adopted country. But many of these items — broadly categorized as health products, food, or medicine — fall under the jurisdiction of the ministry of health (or its equivalent). So, in addition to the import tax (which is levied by customs, a different department), you may have to deal with your package being held at a distant location until you confirm (to the ministry of health) the exact contents of the package.

Here's how this works in Italy: the package arrives in Italy and is held by the ministry of health in Milan. They send you paperwork (by mail) saying they have your package and asking you to describe its exact contents. You then fax or mail that paperwork back to them (often the fax number is busy all day long, so postal mail is the only way). Once they receive it, they determine whether the contents are allowable. If they have a question, they may open the package to see if it really is what you say it is. Then, they either send the package back to its sender (if they do not approve of the contents), or send it on to you. **This whole process can take a couple of weeks, so it's important to tell the sender not to send anything that could spoil or expire. It is also not advisable for them to send anything of significant or sentimental value.** Depending on the length of your term abroad, it may be safer just to avoid having packages mailed to you altogether.

Finally, medicines (over the counter and prescription) follow this same general rule, but are much more at risk for being confiscated, for obvious reasons. If you need a specific medicine, the best first step is to try to find it, or an equivalent, in country. For more on obtaining medicines while abroad, revisit the chapter on health and well-being.

IMMIGRATION

Talking about immigration processes may feel out of place in a chapter that otherwise seems to focus on "going about your daily life." I mention it here because in my experience, it falls under the umbrella of "things I never had to worry about at home that now cause stress or loss of free time."

The process of being legally approved and accepted as a temporary resident during your studies is coordinated by your host country's immigration department. While I can't make country-specific recommendations, I can give you a few general guidelines that will help lessen the stress and (maybe) save you some time:

- Create a reliable method for keeping track of all documentation and appointments related to your immigration status.

- When you have in-person appointments, show up early. As early as you possibly can.

- For in-person appointments, bring water, a snack, and something to do. Even if you show up early, you might be there all day.

- Before submitting documents or going to an in-person appointment, be sure you know exactly which documents you're supposed to bring. Have originals and copies.

- Treat everyone with whom you interact with the utmost respect and deference. This should be a given, but the process can be frustrating, and allowing your frustration to show with immigration officers could mean a negative or long-delayed result.

BUYING GROCERIES & FEEDING YOURSELF

If your living situation includes board, then you won't need to worry too much about food, other than when you want to go out to eat. But if you're cooking for yourself, you'll probably have some limitations, like:

- A smaller refrigerator, so you can keep less food on hand

- Ingredients you'd like to have that are unavailable

- Ingredients available that you don't recognize or know how to use

- Food costs higher than you're accustomed to

- Having to carry all your purchases on a bus ride or walk from stores/markets to home

- Not being able to find everything you need in one location

These limitations can add up to making it feel like a full-time job just to keep yourself fed! You might have to visit a butcher, a farmer's market, and a traditional grocery store to get everything you need, and they might not be in proximity to each other or your home base.

Here are a few tips to manage your menus with ease:

Ask locals where they shop. Sometimes the best markets are smaller, off the beaten path, and you'd never find them without local help. But at these same markets, you can become a regular. Make friends with the vendors, show up frequently over time, and see how much easier shopping becomes!

Buy incrementally. Find grocers or markets on or near the routes you travel each day. Stop in and pick up a few things every time you pass by, and you'll avoid having to spend hours traipsing around town just to get your fridge filled.

Take a cooking class. Any city with even moderate tourism should have a cooking school with cooking classes available to the general public. Some classes are even designed to introduce you to the city's market, where a chef points out ingredients and teaches you how to ask for and purchase them. In the cooking class itself, you'll learn how to make some local dishes, and you'll have the attention of one or more experts, so you can ask about any ingredients you've seen in stores and don't understand how to cook.

Talk to owners and employees of restaurants, cafes, and coffee shops. When you eat out, make a point to talk to the people who work at the eatery, especially if it's small and family-owned. Just like at the markets, becoming a regular has its privileges. Once the staff get to know you, you might find that the prices decrease, or you get larger portions, or free extras. If you love a dish, ask about the recipe! Proud cooks may even be willing to tell you how they made it, or point you to the best source for the ingredients.

WORKING ABROAD

If you actively look for jobs for native English speakers, make local connections early in your term abroad, or just get lucky, you might be offered a part-time job. Working abroad can create opportunities to understand the culture in a deeper way and to get to know more locals than you otherwise would, not to mention having a fantastic venue in which to practice your language skills. If you are interested in working, I would encourage you to start looking for a job as soon as you've settled in, as the hiring process can be subject to bureaucratic delays. You will also need to check with your program administrator regarding the legality of working for pay. The limits (or exclusions) for hiring foreign students vary by country and by industry. You might not be legal to work at all, or there may be a cap on the number of hours you can work, and working illegally can result in penalties as harsh as deportation.

CHAPTER 6

Why Do They Do It That Way?

Learning about "The Way Things Work" and "The Way People Behave" in different countries and on different continents is (I hope!) a major motivator for you to study abroad. The chance to experience another culture from

> **Travel makes one modest. You see what a tiny place you occupy in the world.**
> **-Gustave Flaubert**

within, and over a long stretch of time, offers significant opportunities for learning in ways you can only imagine now. From the first moments in your new home, you'll take note of how things are different from what you're used to, and how they are the same. As these differences occur to you, try to reframe thoughts like "That's weird!" or "Don't they know there's a better way to do this?" Remember that The Way Things Work has evolved, in any culture, over centuries if not millennia, and that there's a complex tapestry of attitudes, experiences, beliefs, historical events, and recent events that inform how a culture looks and feels at any given point in its history (including now).

Your job, as a learner abroad, is both to be open and receptive to differences, and — this is important — to begin to get some insight into *your own* culture. Sometimes this happens for the first time when students are abroad, because (like a fish removed from its bowl) you can only see what surrounds you, how it affects you, and how it has made you who you are, when you're able to see it from an external perspective. Being removed from your own culture and immersed in another gives you that external perspective. The question is, will you use the time to take a good look, or will you hold your breath and wait until you can return to your bowl?

Feeling your way through your own cultural identity and the culture and norms of your home base abroad can be a bumpy road. Just one negative interaction — with a person or a system — can be scary enough to send you back into your comfortable worldview and keep you from appreciating and investigating the true growth available to you during the study abroad experience. While I can't name every possible trigger in this scenario, there are some that are fairly predictable. If you can be prepared at least for those, you'll have a good chance of building up your "expanded worldview" muscles before encountering a critical incident that could otherwise have sent you reeling.

This chapter aims to bring to your attention some of the major cultural and procedural norms that you may experience for the first time as an American living outside the U.S., and to help you prepare to handle them gracefully.

AMERICAN IDENTITY

If you've lived all of your life in the U.S., and you went from high school to college to study abroad without joining the military or traveling outside the U.S., you've probably never been judged harshly on the basis of your nationality. That's about to change. Even if you've never thought or uttered the phrase "America is the greatest nation on Earth!" (and if you have, please see the sidebar), people you meet will see you as a representative of the U.S., and attach to you all of the negative and positive perspectives they hold about the U.S.

Europeans who have not visited the U.S. before have a few common sources of information from which to formulate their opinions of the U.S. and Americans. One is the news, and the American stories that actually make the news in, say, Belgium, are by and large stories of natural disaster, tragedy, violence, war, and anything extreme or outrageous enough to capture attention of people who have no direct stake in the matter. Then there are movies and television. Think of any American television show (especially reality TV), and ask yourself if you'd want someone to develop his or her primary opinions about the U.S. (and, by association, about you) based on that show. A final source is exposure to other Americans, whether they were tourists, expats living in their country, or students who have studied abroad before you. Some people you meet may have had great experiences and relationships with Americans, so they may be pre-disposed to like you, or at least give you the benefit of the doubt. Unfortunately, a more likely scenario is that they have seen drunk, disrespectful students come and go through their town, and tourists who are trying to get the most food/drink/experiences for the least investment (financial and otherwise).

Expat (n.) *slang*: short for *expatriate*, a person who lives outside their native country.

If you only speak English, that's another piece of your American identity that may reinforce a negative stereotype. In most European countries, second-language education begins in primary school, and by the time students are 17 or 18 years old, they speak **at least** two languages (also commonly, three) **in addition to** their native language. This educational practice not only creates a continent of people who are accustomed to speaking their non-native languages frequently; it also creates societies in which people cannot imagine only speaking one language. My dear friend Patrick often described learning a second language as "breaking the stranglehold of English on your consciousness." This is a tough concept to process if you are monolingual, but once you start learning a second language, you realize that it actually opens up the way you think. Many Americans never experience this personal expansion because they remain monolingual. I'd imagine if you'd been learning non-native languages since you were seven years old, as is the case with many Europeans, your mental and emotional expansion would have a big head start on Americans who start to learn at a later age, or not at all.

ATTITUDES AND CUSTOMS

Europe is an entire continent with many distinct cultures (some that align with national borders and some that do not), so there's no generalizing when it comes to The Way Things Are. However, there are some categories in which you can look out for expectations that are different from those at home, and that differ from culture to culture within Europe.

PUNCTUALITY

In general, in northern European cultures, punctuality is important and failing to be punctual is a sign of disrespect to your co-workers or friends. Conversely, in some southern European cultures, meeting times seem to be treated more as suggestions than anything else, and it's generally accepted that the party or dinner actually begins something like 90 minutes after the stated time. (And the stated time might be stated as "around 8:00" which, to an American might mean "somewhere between 7:45 and 8:15" but to a Catalonian might mean "absolutely not before 10:00.") You'll learn the unspoken rules of punctuality in the place where you live, but you might avoid some embarrassment or a long wait if you ask a local to give you a tip from the beginning.

HYGIENE & SERVICE STANDARDS

Again, this category cannot be meaningfully discussed with broad strokes, but in general, Americans are germophobes compared to Europeans. You may have heard stories similar to this one: An American tourist orders a salad in Paris. She finds a clump of dirt in her lettuce, and complains to the waiter. The waiter's response, incredulous that this was even worth mentioning, is something like "Well, what do you expect? It grows in the ground!"

While I don't have personal knowledge of this actually having happened, I'd be surprised if it hasn't (and more than once). It highlights two American cultural norms that may create unrealistic expectations on the part of Americans in Europe: an obsession with being "sanitary" and a high value placed on "customer service."

If it had been a European diner who found dirt on his lettuce, he would have just picked it out, or thrown out that piece of lettuce. You'll never see a European carrying a personal bottle of hand sanitizer. In some regions, Europeans do not use underarm deodorant or antiperspirant (if that bothers you, search online for all the problems that can be caused by putting aluminum and other metals into your body daily for an entire life). The American fixation on being "sanitary" is relatively new from a cultural point of view, and, some would argue, has been driven mostly by corporations wanting to sell cleaning and health products, rather than by an actual need for said products. (Research shows that children who grow up exposed to more germs have more robust immune systems, for starters.)

When you make a purchase in Europe, your ability to return the item post-purchase (if that option is available at all) will be much more strictly limited than it is in the U.S. Even if a shop does accept returns, it may only be for store credit and not for a refund. Sales clerks may not be in the habit of processing returns and may not be thrilled if you initiate one.

Most service-industry employees (unlike in the U.S.) work for a living wage, so their salary is not dependent on your tips, and therefore not dependent on them treating you like you are the most important person in the store/restaurant/world. I'm not suggesting that servers will be rude or inadequate; I'm saying they will (as they should) see themselves as your equal, and will not stand for anything other than pleasant and dignified treatment from your end.

THE ELEVATOR IS NOT A SOCIAL CLUB (ALSO, YOU TALK TOO LOUD)

In general, Americans tend to share more about their lives, sooner after meeting people, than Europeans do. The classic example is of an American getting into an elevator with Europeans who then have heard the American's life story by the time the elevator ride ends. In my experience, though, Americans are even more likely to *ask questions* — questions that seem inappropriate to Europeans who don't know you at all — than to start talking about themselves. Either way, it's not culturally comfortable to many Europeans to strike up conversation with others just because you happen to be sharing the same public space. **This doesn't mean you can't do it;** it means you should pay attention to how people react if you do, and adjust accordingly.

A detail that many Americans do not notice at first: the volume at which you naturally speak is likely much higher than that of the average European. Combined with not speaking the local language, or, at best, speaking it with an accent, your loud volume will draw attention to you in public places. There's nothing inherently wrong with that, but be mindful of what's going on around you and your role in the scene. Dozens of times, I have been on a train that was filled with all kinds of people in transit. Most of them were reading, quietly conversing with the people next to them, or working on a computer. And there's one group of Americans talking loudly enough that everyone in the train car becomes an involuntary audience to their conversation rather than being allowed to be at peace with their own thoughts. Situations like these contribute to the generalization that Americans are rude, self-absorbed, and attention-seeking, when in fact those loud-talkers were probably just extremely excited and enthusiastic about the journey they were on. Again, it's just a matter of taking note of what's going on around you and how you fit into the bigger picture.

POLITICALLY CORRECT IS CULTURALLY CONTEXTUAL

The value and nature of political correctness depend to a large degree on the perspective of the person you're engaging. For the purposes of this writing, I would like to break down the term. "Political" comes from a Greek root meaning "community" or "citizen." "Correctness" is a state of being right or true. So, when I talk about political correctness, I'm speaking of the way people in a community express themselves, such that there is general agreement that the mode of expression is right, acceptable, or true. Why is this worth mentioning? You may encounter people who express themselves with words that would be considered rude or discriminatory in your world. The meaning you attach to different words arises from your culture; others may or may not share your understanding of their meaning, or what is implied by their use.

I will never forget the first time I heard a five-year-old Norwegian girl exclaim "shit!" when she dropped something on the floor. I was shocked (and amused), and looked around the room at the other adults for a similar reaction (and to see how she'd be disciplined). But all the other adults were also Norwegian, and they weren't reacting at all. The word holds no stronger meaning for them than *darn* or *phooey*.

As a second example, in many circles in American culture, it is not considered politically correct to use the word "fat" as a descriptor of an individual. If you had this conversation with a friend:

Friend: "Do you know that person on the park bench?"
You: "Which one?
Friend: "The fat one."

you would probably be a little bit shocked, and you might even suggest that your friend could have said "The one in the blue jacket" or "the one with the shorter hair" instead. But the lack of ease around the word "fat" is not objective; it's created in U.S. culture because we believe that there is something wrong with being fat. But in some cultures, "fat" is just a word like any other adjective — skinny, tall, short, redhead, cute, plain, fat. All just words used to describe people. The point here is that you may be surprised at what people say without judgment, or at things they take offense to that you never would have anticipated. Speak with kindness and listen with an open mind.

PROUDLY PATRIOTIC?

Patriotism in Europe does not look like patriotism in the U.S. That's not to say that Europeans aren't proud of who they are, their cultural heritage, and their fellow citizens. But these attitudes exist in a more tempered state than they do in [at least some circles in] the U.S. National pride in Europe is much more impassioned during FIFA matches than in the course of a conversation at the pub on the corner.

In general, in my experience, Europeans take a much more nuanced perspective on their government's policies and actions, rarely supporting or renouncing them across the board. So, if you find yourself in a conversation about global politics, and your perspective sounds something like, "The U.S. is the best because we have freedom!" — expect to be challenged. Your loyalty to and pride in your country may be remarkable to some Europeans. They may want to understand it better, and may try to accomplish that by asking you to explain why you are so loyal and proud. They will also probably know more about the role of the U.S. in global events than you know about their country's, which means that if you want to have a meaningful conversation, you need to know what the U.S. is doing and has done, both at home and out in the world.

"AMERICA IS THE GREATEST NATION ON EARTH!"

You may or may not have expressed this sentiment, but at a minimum, you've probably heard it. If you haven't done so before, take a moment to ponder:

- Why is this important?

- Why might someone feel the need to say this?

- How might this sound to people from one of the other 200-ish countries in the world?

And as you ruminate on that last question, consider these points of information:

- The infant mortality rate in the U.S. places us somewhere around 45th in the global rankings. Most of the European countries are ahead of us.

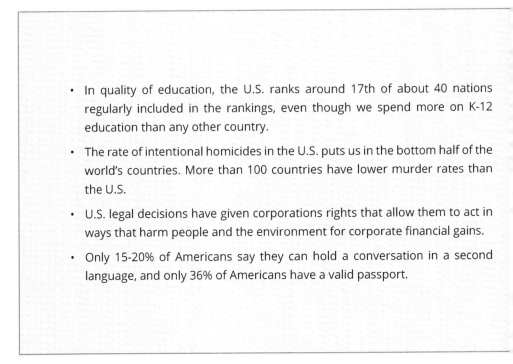

- In quality of education, the U.S. ranks around 17th of about 40 nations regularly included in the rankings, even though we spend more on K-12 education than any other country.

- The rate of intentional homicides in the U.S. puts us in the bottom half of the world's countries. More than 100 countries have lower murder rates than the U.S.

- U.S. legal decisions have given corporations rights that allow them to act in ways that harm people and the environment for corporate financial gains.

- Only 15-20% of Americans say they can hold a conversation in a second language, and only 36% of Americans have a valid passport.

VARIOUS AND SUNDRY OTHER DIFFERENCES

Showing and Carrying ID

Your ID is required by law in more situations in Europe than it is in the U.S. Furthermore, because you won't have a national ID from the country you'll be living in, your passport is the only valid form of ID you'll have. Please note: your state-issued driver's license is not valid as a form of ID. Even if you rent a car, you will also have to show your passport. Handing over your passport can feel very vulnerable when you know that you can't get on a plane and get home without it, but you will have to use it frequently. When you check into hotels, not only will you have to show your passport, but often they will take it from you and return it to you that night or the next day, because they are legally obligated to register you as a guest by copying information from your passport into their system. If you get a SIM card to use in your cell phone, or pay to use internet access at an internet café, you'll likely have to show your passport; under certain circumstances, it's required by anti-pornography and anti-terrorism laws.

In many countries, you are required by law to carry ID on your person at all times. Since your only valid ID is your passport, this creates a dilemma: carry it with you all the time and create a higher likelihood of its getting lost or stolen, or keep it safe at home but be out of compliance? While I will not advise you to break the law, I will say that losing your passport — especially in a location without an American embassy or consulate — can be expensive and disruptive. Carrying a color copy of your passport's photo page in addition to a driver's license is one way of walking the line between risk of loss and law-abiding.

Price & Availability

In many restaurants, cafés, and bars, it costs more to sit at a table than it does to take your food/drink to go or consume it while standing at the bar. In Italy, in areas highly-trafficked by tourists, a shot of espresso can cost €0.90 at the bar but five times that if you sit at a table to consume the exact same beverage. These price differences may be prominently displayed, but can often come as a surprise, so be sure to look carefully for two sets of prices on the menu, or for a note indicating what the upcharge is for "table service."

In most parts of Europe, stores aren't open late into the evening, and 24-hour stores are exceptionally rare. Department stores can close as early as 6:00pm; in some countries there's one weekday (often Thursday) on which they stay open later, perhaps until 9:00. Supermarkets and smaller grocers hold similar operating hours, and many are still closed on Sundays, or perhaps open one or two Sundays per month. The variety of things available in stores will also be much more limited. Museums and other cultural attractions are typically closed one day per week, so check ahead before you plan an outing.

Public Policy

This is a topic broad enough for its own series of books, but some policies are more applicable to you, a visiting foreigner, than others. For instance, different countries handle emergency situations differently. If you are judged to be a danger to yourself or others, you could be hospitalized against your will, and held until doctors in that hospital believe you are well enough to be released. If you do something that is against the law and get arrested, no one — not your parents, not the American Embassy — can erase the consequences of what you did, or affect the outcome of a trial in any way. Remember that as a visitor to any country, it is your responsibility to respect that country's sovereignty by knowing and abiding by their laws. The laws of the U.S. — and your rights as a U.S. citizen — are irrelevant. I've heard too many stories of American students who, in a situation that could have gone either way, ended up in hot water with local law enforcement because they exclaimed, "I'm an American citizen! I have rights!"

Traffic Differences

If you'll be driving at all, it's important to know differences in signage, rules of the road, speed limits, and conventions of driving that may not be in the rule book but that everyone honors. Even if you won't be driving, you will definitely be a pedestrian, and it's important to know some fundamentals of driving culture in your home away from home. It's a great idea to do a quick search online to be sure you know who has the right of way and how the most common traffic signs look.

Differences of Measure

Europeans use the metric system, measuring distance in meters/kilometers, weight in grams/kilograms, and temperature in degrees Celsius. While you can use an app or cheat sheet to convert from Imperial to metric or Fahrenheit to Celsius, it's pretty easy just to learn a few guidelines that will help you become comfortable with using the other systems without needing to translate.

For Temperature

A rough model is to take the Celsius temperature, double it, and add 30. This is more accurate in the middle and less accurate at the extremes, but it's better than having no idea. And if you combine it with a few paired conversions that are easy to remember, you'll be in good shape:

- 37 Celsius is 98.6 Fahrenheit (normal body temperature)
- 28 Celsius is 82 Fahrenheit
- 16 Celsius is 61 Fahrenheit
- 10 Celsius is 50 Fahrenheit
- 00 Celsius is 32 Fahrenheit (you probably already learned this one in school)

If you memorize these few pairs, and the formula above, you'll start to understand temperature in Celsius in no time.

For Distance

If you're a runner or racer, you have a head start on this one. You probably know that a mile is about 1.6km, and a 5k is about 3.1 miles. A 10k run is 6.2 miles. With those numbers in mind, you can always do the math pretty quickly for any distance just by adding 10's (6.2mi), 100's (62mi), 1000's (620mi), 5's (3.1mi), and 50's (31mi). For example, 250km is 100+100+50km, or two 100's (124mi) and one 50 (31mi), so about 155 miles.

For Shorter Distances

An inch is about 2.5cm, so ten inches is about 25cm. You probably won't need detailed understanding of lengths in centimeters or millimeters, but for added confidence, measure your own index finger from tip to base in centimeters, and memorize that number as a basic point of reference.

For Weight

One kilogram is about 2.2lbs. So a half kilo (500 grams) is about a pound. At lower weights (like for buying meat or cheese at the market), you can just ignore that decimal and consider 500 grams to be a pound (it's no tragedy if you get 0.1 pounds more cheese than you needed, right?). At heavier weights, or when you need to be more precise, the conversion is pretty easy:

• From kilos to pounds, double the kg number and then add ten percent of the doubled number to itself (so, 40 kilos doubled is 80. 80 plus ten percent of 80 is 88).

• From pounds to kilos, divide the lbs number in half, then subtract ten percent (so, 250 lbs divided in half is 125, minus ten percent — 12.5 — is 112.5).

These numbers are not what you'd get with a conversion calculation, since 1 kg = 2.20462 lb, but they are close enough for most purposes. In the workbook, I've included a "conversions cheat sheet" that covers all of these calculations again in a format that may be easier to read.

To conclude this chapter, I offer a series of questions I used to pose to my students when they first arrived in Europe. Knowledge of the local culture and customs was at its lowest point, and would only increase from there. But in those first weeks, it's easy to make a mistake because of a norm you're unaware of or a custom you don't understand. These questions, however, do not require any culture-specific knowledge. Whenever you are unsure whether it's okay to proceed, ask yourself, "What if everyone in my presence were following my lead right now? What if they were all doing what I am doing? Would things be better, or worse?"

CHAPTER 7

Traveling from Your Home-Base

You're making a big trip, across an ocean (maybe two?), and right now that probably seems like "the travel" you'll be doing. But once you arrive and settle in, especially if you're going to Europe, your study abroad

> **All journeys have secret destinations of which the traveler is unaware.**
> **-Martin Buber**

destination — which I am calling your *home-base* — will quickly become "home," and the prospect of visiting other cities, regions, and countries will be extremely appealing. Americans studying in Europe have used their semesters abroad as a chance to see more of the continent for decades. While the most popular mode of transportation has changed (from hitchhiking to rail passes to low-cost airlines), the ubiquity of students abroad on trips-within-The-Trip has not. If you've never planned your own travel before, or never planned multiple trips in the space of just a few months, then you can easily get overwhelmed by reservations, deposits, coordinating multiple modes of transportation, and the like.

Travel is full of unpredictable twists and turns, with a snafu thrown in here and there. This chapter aims to help you avoid creating any of those yourself, so you can save your energy for all the ones that are beyond your control.

CHOOSING LOCATIONS AND CRAFTING A SCHEDULE

The allure of checking dozens of countries off your bucket list can be strong, but remember that you're studying where you're studying for a reason. Don't plan so many days away from your home-base that you end up finishing your term abroad without having developed connections in, and a good understanding of, your home-base.

As you plan your travel, the first thing to consider is your academic schedule. If you don't have access to syllabi and academic requirements before departure, then you can make tentative plans, but don't finalize or pay for anything! Imagine booking your dream weekend trip to Munich, only to discover that there's a mandatory academic check-in on Friday afternoon, and you'll lose your student status if you don't attend. It may seem a harsh example, but remember, you're **studying** abroad. If traveling is more important to you, I promise it's much cheaper to backpack on your own for a month or two in the summer than to use a semester abroad as a convenient excuse to see more of the world.

Once you're clear about your program's requirements (including any required trips), think about your top two destinations. If you only got to travel twice during the semester abroad, where would you go? Are there weekends that would afford you a longer stay in these places? For example, are there local or national holidays that your school observes — or even American holidays, if observed — that create 3- or 4-day weekends? Are you able to arrive at your home base early, or (even better) stay for a week or two after the semester ends? Look for the possibilities. Although Europe is very accessible even for short trips, every extra day you can squeeze in gives you so many more opportunities to see and do new things.

If you're staying for a semester, I'd advise planning no more than three trips before you leave the U.S. Many of your fellow students will also be traveling, and if you've already booked yourself solid, you might miss out on chances to travel with someone you meet after arriving in-country (and who, for example, has friends or family hosting them for free). And certainly there will be destinations that are not on your radar now, but that will be once you have spent a few weeks in your new home. Leaving most of your weekends free also keeps you open to the possibility that you'll love your home abroad so much that you won't want to leave at all!

TRAVELING SOLO

There are countless resources available online regarding traveling solo (a search for "tips for traveling alone" will turn up rich and diverse material). While I believe it's an extraordinary learning experience, and something everyone should do at some point in life, it's also true that if you're traveling alone and something happens to you (whether it's a broken foot, losing your passport/credit cards, or getting mugged), it will be much more difficult to navigate your way home. You can take reasonable precautions to reduce your chances of being in these situations, but they're not 100% preventable. Only you can know whether you're ready to travel alone. For many students, the first time abroad is not the right time to try traveling alone. It's not your last chance, so don't worry if you'd rather stick with a group. If you do try traveling solo, be sure you're comfortable with the risks you are taking, and communicate clearly with your loved ones, so they'll know where you are throughout your trip.

BOOKING FLIGHTS

The options available to you for flying around Europe are numerous, and they can be confusing. The airlines (and flights) you choose will depend on your personal preferences, your schedule, and where you want to strike the balance of convenience versus cost. The first decision you'll make is between so-called "major carriers" (the ones that are members of Star Alliance, SkyTeam, oneworld, etc.) and the so-called "low-cost" airlines (like EasyJet, RyanAir, WizzAir, and many, many more). I use "so-called" in both cases because some of the low-cost airlines have grown so large that they really are major carriers (even without an alliance), and because whether a flight ends up being "low-cost" depends on many factors other than which airline you fly.

Should you buy tickets as soon as you know where and when you want to travel? It's hard to know. Airline fares are unpredictable. Sometimes, prices get consistently higher as you get closer to the travel date. Other times, fares drop sometime between when you've decided where you're going and your actual travel date. The most important point I can make about booking flights is that you should do a little research before paying for anything. This way, you will avoid hidden costs and surprise fees. If you find a flight you want and see that the number of seats available is low, you should go ahead and book it.

Some good clearinghouse sites for finding airfare are www.kayak.com, www.traveleurope.com, www.momondo.com, and www.skyscanner.com. These sites will help you compare flights offered by major carriers. (Kayak will also predict, when possible, whether the price of a flight is expected to increase or decrease in the coming days.) Then there are the low-cost airlines, which often fly from airports near but not in your desired destination, and whose flights are not indexed by most clearinghouse sites, meaning you have to visit each of their sites directly (sites like www.easyjet.com, www.ryanair.com, and www.wizzair.com).

Caveat: there are also clearinghouse websites in the local language, and they may offer fares lower than what you find elsewhere. Be sure that you are able to understand the fine print on these sites, and that you **read it**. Some of these sites require a second-step verification before your booking is final. If you receive an email from them in a language you don't know well, you may miss the part where you have to reply in some way in order to have your ticket booked. I have known students who showed up at the airport with bags packed, only to find they had no reservation because they had never confirmed their ticket purchase.

If you travel with a low-cost airline, fares can be much, much lower than they are on major carriers (sometimes, as low as €5 before taxes). However, please factor in the additional time and cost of transport from your town to the departure airport, and from the arrival airport to your final destination.

Remember that low-cost airlines often fly in and out of the minor airports in a region, not the major airport you think of when you think of a particular city. For example, Brussels Airport is just about 10km (15 minutes on the train) from the city center, but Charleroi, the airport used by low-cost airlines for "Brussels" flights, is 60km (more than an hour on a bus) from the city center.

In many cases, you will still save more by booking the low-cost flight, as the cost of the additional transportation is less than the fare difference — but you might also lose many hours of time you could use exploring your destination. In general, local train tickets and airport shuttles are readily available, so you don't usually have to worry about booking them along with your flight. You can buy them after you've arrived at the airport (this also avoids the possibility of losing the value of a fixed-schedule ticket because your flight arrived late).

If you are using a combination of flights and buses/trains to save money, pay special attention to the arrival and departure times of your flights, so that you don't find yourself stuck because your flight times don't correspond with bus, train, or shuttle times. I cannot emphasize this strongly enough; if, for example, your final destination is Bruges, and you intend to fly to Brussels and then take a train to Bruges, where you have booked lodging, be sure that there is enough time after your flight lands to make your way to the train station and catch the train. Otherwise, you may end up spending a night in the train station or airport because you've missed the last train of the day. Meanwhile, the lodging you've already paid for sits empty in Bruges.

Another thing to keep in mind, especially if you are planning on using budget airlines, is that it is sometimes cheaper to travel using one-way tickets from two different airlines. It all depends on how much time you want to spend testing out different configurations, and how high your tolerance is for managing the details of a complicated itinerary.

LODGING

The options for lodging have opened up with the advent of sharing-economy sites like Airbnb and Couchsurfing, and consolidator/coupon sites like Hotwire and Groupon. The basic choices boil down to: hotel, hostel, campsite, private home. Each has its advantages and disadvantages, risks and rewards.

HOTELS

Hotels generally offer the highest level of services and features, central location, and at least the presumption of safety and security. They also have more rigid rules than most of the other types of lodging, and can be significantly more expensive. However, there are ways to get hotel rooms more cheaply than you might expect. For example:

- Accrue points through a fidelity program (more on this later) and use them for discounts, upgrades, or free rooms.

- Try Hotwire (hotwire.com). Though you can't be sure exactly which hotel you'll end up in, you can see the rating and the area of town in which it's located, along with reviews from others who've stayed there. Hotwire can afford you significant discounts off the cheapest rate available otherwise, but once you book, you've paid and it's non-refundable, so be sure before you click "buy."

- Regularly scan Groupon for the places you want to visit. Often you'll find packages available that include modest hotels and some activities, for a modest price.

- If you speak the language (or live with someone who does), call small hotels and try to negotiate directly with the staff. If their occupancy is low for the days you want, you might be surprised. This can be even more effective if you're traveling with a large group. If you have at least 10 people traveling, call and ask to talk to someone about a group rate, or inquire by email.

HOSTELS

Hostels can vary dramatically in quality, safety, services, and price. Hostels located in prime real estate in the center of town can often get away with very low quality and very high prices, while further out you might find spacious, beautiful hostels at much lower rates. And, there are lots of gems that are a good balance of location, price, and quality. Some useful consolidator sites are hostelworld.com, hostelbookers.com, and hostels.com. Here you'll find comprehensive information on amenities, lots of photos, lots of user reviews, and the ability to book directly from the sites in some cases.

Staying in hostels can be a wonderful experience, because they tend to attract people who are interested in meeting other travelers and up for coordinating activities with newly-made friends on the fly. Hostel staff will also generally go out of their way to help you get access to whatever you're looking for in your destination. Just a couple of caveats: the quality of (some) hostels has risen dramatically in the past twenty years, and the prices have risen right along with it. Hostels charge per person, not per room, so if you're traveling with a group, this is something to consider. Also, sleeping in a room with ten beds filled with strangers (who might behave in ways you wouldn't) and having to leave the room to use the toilet or shower isn't for everyone. Compare and contrast hostels with other lodging options before you commit.

CAMPSITES

Campsites are widely available throughout Europe, but most are only open during months in which the weather is warm. Camping facilities and pricing cover a wide range, depending on the country you're visiting and the individual campground. How much (if any) equipment you need to bring yourself is also highly variable. If you're a dedicated camper and wish to camp around Europe, I recommend exploring campingeurope.com.

PRIVATE HOMES

Even if you don't have personal connections to rely on, you can now stay in private homes because of sites like Airbnb, Couchsurfing, and VRBO. Depending on which accommodation you choose, this type of lodging can be more expensive than the most expensive hotel, cheaper than a hostel, or even free. The risk of staying in private homes is highest, because you don't know what you're getting until you arrive. There are no meaningful controls in terms of safety and security, you can't be sure the place will be clean and bedbug-free, and if you arrive and you don't like what you see, you can't just ask to be moved to a different room. On the other hand, you could meet great people who are willing to be knowledgeable local guides during your stay and who become lifelong friends. If you're considering staying in private homes, be sure to select locations that have multiple positive user reviews, check the site's safety standards and policy on dealing with emergencies, and — especially the first time — travel and stay with a friend rather than alone.

BONUS CATEGORY: TRAVEL AS LODGING

If you're able to combine lodging and travel, you can sometimes increase the amount of time you get to spend in your destination while decreasing your costs. Both trains and boats can provide opportunities to spend your sleep hours traveling, and wake up in your destination, ready to explore. In both cases, you will pay more to reserve a bed than just to book a seat on the train/boat, so be sure to figure that into your cost comparison versus other modes of transportation.

Furthermore, especially with trains, you want to confirm that you won't have to get off the train and switch to another one at a time that will disrupt your sleep. Finally, arriving early in the morning can be daunting if you're not able to check in to your lodging until late afternoon, and you're still in the clothes you slept in.

POINTS FOR FIDELITY

Before you depart the U.S., enroll in the frequent flyer programs of each of the major airline alliances. This won't cost you anything, and just being a member may sometimes afford you benefits that non-members miss out on. If you already have a preferred alliance, check to see how/if it cooperates with hotel groups. Some alliances allow you to earn airline miles for hotel stays, or vice versa. Finally, get a credit card that doesn't impose fees for international purchases and allows you to accrue points to be used toward travel, then use it for every possible expense. Most credit card companies offer a card like this, and which one you choose will depend on your preferences, travel style, and credit history. While some cards allow you to earn more points than others, the biggest gap is between earning some points and no points. So don't let the thousands of dollars you'll spend while abroad go unacknowledged by the points people!

MISCELLANEOUS OTHER TIPS

1. When you travel somewhere for the weekend, or longer, look into transport passes for local buses, trams, or subways. Often you can save by buying a 1-day pass, multiple day pass, or booklet of tickets all at once, rather than buying single tickets for every ride.

2. Read labels and signs before standing in line at a museum, transport hub, event venue, really anywhere. Often there are separate lines for patrons in particular categories, or seeking particular products. Avoid spending 30 minutes in a line only to find out that you were in the wrong one by politely walking to the front and reading notices at each window until you understand whether they are all equal, or some will get you what you want faster than others.

3. Many private companies offer weekend trips that are inclusive of travel (by bus), lodging (in hostels), and some activities and/or meals. Some students use these companies exclusively for their travel while in Europe. At the risk of making enemies, I'm going to advise against this. Traveling with a group of 50 to 250 other American students essentially takes away your ability to explore the destination, see it with your own eyes, and learn about yourself and your own travel style. If your group fills the hostel to capacity, you won't meet travelers from other countries that weekend. If you're always with a big group of English speakers, you'll miss the chance to interact with locals, or be seen as anything more than a tourist among tourists. Furthermore, these companies operate to make profit, and if — even days before departure — they determine that a trip will not be profitable, they will cancel it. You'll get your money back, but it could be too late or too expensive to make new arrangements.

4. Proceed with caution when considering participating in adventurous experiences like skiing, spelunking, bungee jumping, sky diving, para-gliding, and the like. Although regulation in Europe is strong, and operators are highly likely to provide the safest possible equipment and conditions, accidents

can always happen. Your insurance may not cover injuries sustained in anything they label "high-risk" activities.

5. Transportation strikes occur with some regularity throughout Europe. There's not much you can do to avoid them, but you should pay attention to local and national news so you know they're coming (they're usually announced). If you are traveling and a strike prevents you from getting back home, it's better to know ahead of time so that you can try to make arrangements for a new flight, rather than showing up at the airport with hundreds of other stranded travelers.

TRAVELING IN TODAY'S WORLD

At publication time, the frequency of terrorist incidents in Europe is on the rise. While no one can predict with certainty the location or timing of a terrorist attack, travelers can take proactive steps to increase their chances of staying safe. The U.S. State Department's website (travel.state.gov) has an entire section for students abroad, where you can find out more about your destination, including likelihood of terrorist attacks, crime statistics, and potential for natural disasters, as well as tips on how to stay safe. You'll also find a link there to STEP, the Smart Traveler Enrollment Program, which offers U.S. citizens traveling abroad the opportunity to register their trip with the nearest embassy or consulate. You should do this. (I haven't used absolute terms very often in this book, but here, I must.) It only takes a few minutes, and as a result, you'll receive helpful information from that embassy or consulate that may impact your travel plans. Being registered with STEP also helps the embassy and your family reach you in an emergency situation.

Another feature of the state department's website is the "alerts and warnings" section, linked from the home page. Here you'll find warnings about travel to specific countries, with explanations and advice about whether Americans should travel there. When traveling to another country from your home-base, always check to see if the state department has issued an alert or warning that includes that country, so that you can make a well-informed decision.

Before you travel, you'll also want to have considered what could happen if you are in a city when a terrorist attack occurs. Even if you aren't impacted directly in the attack itself, significant trickle-down effects are almost certain. This could mean panic in the streets, shutdown of local transportation, shutdown of international transportation (especially if the attack occurs in an airport or train station), strong police presence on the streets, curfew, inability to communicate because of overloaded cell towers or internet channels, and the list could go on and on. While I hope you won't experience any of this during your term abroad, it's important to acknowledge it as a possibility, and think about how you'll respond if it does occur.

IN SUMMARY

Traveling from your home-base while living abroad is an amazing opportunity for you to get to see more of Europe than you might ever, under any other circumstances. Seize that opportunity, but remember that the opportunity of living abroad is even greater. Find a balance of travel and exploration of your home base that feels right for you. And even if you never travel alone, make a point to spend at least a few hours alone in every destination. You'll discover things — about the destination and about yourself — that you never would have discovered if you hadn't had the courage to venture off on your own.

CHAPTER 8

Staying Safe, Secure, and Sane

Whether you have ever had occasion to use it or not, an intricate and sometimes imperceptible safety net surrounds and supports you when you're at home. This safety net has different components for

> **Don't do what you know on a gut level to be the wrong thing to do.**
> -Cheryl Strayed

each individual, but you can probably think of at least a few pieces that make up your safety net off the top of your head. They might include:

- parents and/or family

- close friends

- co-workers and/or your boss

- access to money (bank account/credit card)

- a smartphone

There are dozens of other components of your safety net that you might not ever think of (before living abroad, that is), but that can be just as critical to your safety and/or sanity. These may include, and are not limited to:

- a general understanding of what is legal and illegal

- being given the benefit of the doubt if you do something inappropriate
- an ability to communicate fluently and easily with strangers on the street in an emergency
- an ability to communicate fluently and easily with law enforcement
- knowledge of how the health care system works, and the ability to understand and communicate with health care professionals
- the ability to call your doctor's office, describe symptoms, and ask for advice without having to go there
- easy, frequent, cheap access to your family and friends through cell phones and/or the internet
- instincts and intuition about what looks dangerous or safe, built up as you've lived in the culture
- easy, cheap access to food that meets your nutritional needs and avoids allergens or intolerances
- strong regulation of safety in consumer products
- an ability to read and understand posted signs, warnings, and instructions
- a community of others with similar ages and circumstances, so that any problem has probably been solved before and knowledge about solving it is easily crowdsourced
- a general knowledge of how most systems around you work
- a general belief that you know how to navigate your way through the world safely

And these could all be condensed to one basic concept: **safety is in place when you have access to support and you can reliably predict how things will unfold.** When you're abroad, your access to support is reduced, and you cannot always predict how things are going to go. This doesn't mean you're never going to feel safe while abroad. But you will likely feel *more vulnerable* than you do at home, and you'll need to take some proactive measures to increase your chances of feeling safe (and actually *being* safe).

While I'll use the words "safe" and "safety" frequently in this chapter, they stand for a more nuanced set of qualities. It's not just about feeling safe — as in, your life is not in danger and no physical harm will come to you — but in feeling secure, supported, stable, sane (of sound mind and body), healthy, at peace. I'll focus on the more tangible aspects of maintaining your safety, because in those areas it's much easier to give tips and advice that can be useful for anyone. However, mental and emotional security can be much more elusive than physical safety. Read through the lists of the parts of a safety net again, and this time read them with this scenario in mind: it's 4:00AM, your phone has no signal, and you've got a sharp pain in your lower right abdomen. It may not be anything serious, but imagine what happens to your mental and emotional states (while you're also in physical pain) as you consider what's missing from the resources you typically have available to you.

While you can't prevent the unexpected, you can be knowledgeable about how to increase your chances at staying safe and sane, and how to get help when needed. That's what this chapter is about: increasing your awareness to prepare you to better handle critical incidents.

COMMUNICATION & CONNECTION

Despite your best efforts, communication with family and friends from home will be less frequent than you imagine, and probably also more difficult than you imagine. (That's okay. You're going abroad to have an experience for you. Reduced communication during this time is recommended!) If you are in a relationship, communication with your significant other will also be difficult, may be strained at times, and you may feel like your S.O. just doesn't "get" you anymore. If you usually talk to your mom five times a day, that's either going to change, or you're going to miss out on a lot of opportunities while abroad. If you're accustomed to these high levels of communication, over time, you may begin to feel distant or isolated, or homesickness and culture shock may be difficult to overcome. Talk to your loved ones about this before you leave. Talk about realistic expectations for communication, and find ways to focus on the *quality* of your connection, rather than the *quantity* of your communication.

COMMUNICATION IN EMERGENCIES

Regardless of how you work out your day-to-day communication, you'll want to have an agreed-on plan for emergency communication. If you have a smartphone with international access, this should be simple. Decide what warrants a call, and when. If a family member is injured or killed, will you receive a call no matter what time it is? What about if a pet dies? If you have a medical concern, at what level do you send an email or message via social media, and at what level do your loved ones want to hear from you by telephone? If you are hospitalized and unable to contact them yourself, who will do that? It's important to talk to your friends about this possibility as well. If you don't come home from a bar one night, how long will your roommates wait before they alert someone? (Answer: that won't happen, because you'll go home when the last friend goes home.) Will they try to contact you? How many attempts should they make before assuming something has gone wrong? These worst-case-scenarios are not so fun to think about, but having open dialogue before they happen will help everyone involved feel calmer and more certain in an emergency.

If you don't have phone service while abroad, and are relying on the availability of free wifi for emergency communication, you're in a much different situation. In this case, it's **even more important** to communicate frequently with friends and fellow students, and to have clear agreements about not leaving anyone behind when going out, not changing travel plans without notifying others, etc. If at all possible, I would recommend having some level of phone service available, even if only for emergencies.

Pro Tip: In some countries, pay-as-you go plans and inexpensive basic cell phones are available locally. You may be able to find a plan that will provide free incoming calls and texts, charging you only for outgoing calls.

Natural disasters, terrorist attacks, and accidents can occur anywhere, and news spreads lightning-quick. When you're traveling away from your home base, be sure someone at home knows where you are. If you've traveled to London for the weekend, and a bus is bombed in London, get word to your loved ones as soon as possible that you're safe. If you were supposed to be in London but changed plans at the last minute without telling them, make contact to reassure them. And pay attention to the news you're hearing locally, because if something major happens, you can bet that your loved ones will hear about it (and worry), even if it's only vaguely related to your location. For example, several years ago, severe flooding in Italy made international news, and several deaths were reported. Even though the flooding took place in a different part of Italy, parents just saw the news, heard "Italy," and immediately started trying to contact their sons and daughters. Your loved ones will worry when you're thousands of miles away and they know they can't help in a crisis. So, do your best to follow your emergency communication plan, keep them abreast of where and how you are, and let them know you understand their worry.

SAFETY & ALCOHOL

I addressed alcohol consumption already in chapter four, from the perspective of staying healthy and well, and not trading the prospect of meaningful, diverse experiences for the habit of regularly going out drinking with other Americans. Now, I would like to talk about alcohol consumption from this perspective: it could play a significant role in your having a life-altering experience while abroad. In fact, ninety-nine percent of the negative life-altering experiences I witnessed or learned of among American students (both mine and others) studying in Italy were alcohol-related. These included:

- being mugged and beaten up (with resulting skull fracture)
- getting lost walking back to the hostel, arriving too late to enter, and having to sleep outside overnight and fend off would-be attackers
- being sexually assaulted
- being taken to a private home and waking up not knowing where she was
- being accused of and/or involved in a crime (with or without memory of what happened)
- being arrested
- getting drunk and missing flight/train home
- falling from a roof or balcony (to his death)
- drowning
- getting hit by a car
- getting hit by a train

As you might imagine, these traumatic events would change the course of your life (if they don't end it). Some of them were caused 100% by actions taken by the student. Some were vicious attacks where someone else was completely at fault, but the student still suffered. All of them involved a student who was intoxicated. While being mugged or sexually assaulted is **never** the fault of the victim, it is the victim who has to live with the consequences of the assault. And if you can do *anything* to lessen your chances of being a victim (while still enjoying life), I encourage you to do it.

This means not drinking so much that you don't know where you are, or how to get home, or who you came with. It means watching out for others who are drinking, and not being afraid to speak up when you think they've had too much. It means knowing that just as you behave differently when you're drinking, so do others, so caution with people you've just met is sensible. It means stretching your social muscles and daring to try to engage in meaningful conversation without needing to numb yourself with alcohol first.

If you do consume alcohol to an extreme, such that you lose consciousness and have to be hospitalized, you will most certainly be treated differently by health care professionals than you would be in the U.S. Drinking culture in the U.S. is formed by complex, interwoven factors, but in my experience, two have dramatic impact on how intoxicated college students are treated: the "extended adolescence" of students over age 18, and the widespread attitude that "drinking too much is what college students do." In Europe, university is a place where students gather to attend class and take exams. Most universities have no significant population of students living on campus; in fact, many European students continue to live at home and commute to school. So, ad hoc parties in residence halls, frat parties, house parties, and the like are virtually unthinkable in most European educational institutions.

Similarly, when you are an 18-year-old European, you're considered an adult. You're responsible for your own life and for making your own decisions. If you choose to drink so much that you lose consciousness, this may be an indication in some cultures that you are mentally ill, or incapable of taking care of yourself as an adult. At worst, you could be admitted against your will until you can pass a psychological examination. At best, you may be considered irresponsible and reckless, using public resources that are not unlimited and that should be reserved for people who are really ill. In fact, in some European cultures, intoxication may be handled with a shrug and a dismissal ("he's drunk, he can go home and sleep it off"). This may sound harsh, but consider the perspective of an emergency room doctor who sees local (native) patients so intoxicated that they need to be hospitalized perhaps once a year, and visiting Americans in the same condition every weekend. Your best move is to avoid being that American altogether.

AN ABUNDANCE OF CAUTION?

Striking a balance between being open to new experiences and exposing yourself to unsafe situations is one of the most challenging aspects of spending a semester or year abroad. Meeting local people and forging relationships with them can be a major component of your experience (and can accelerate both your academic and personal learning). Some students build friendships that last a lifetime, but even if you don't, the chance to have drinks with a group of local friends and be a part of their conversation in their native language, or to be invited to someone's house for dinner, could offer opportunities you won't get in any other way.

At the same time, there are people in every culture who seek to harm or take advantage of others, and you don't want to expose yourself to danger in the name of getting to know locals, or even "being nice." So, how do you stay safe without closing yourself off to the possibility of getting to know real people who live in the place where you're studying, and can teach you about it from a truly local point of view?

The truth is, there is no way to be sure that you're not befriending someone who means you harm. However, there are many ways to hedge your bets. Start by meeting locals who are vetted in some way; that is, they have been vouched for either by an institution or by someone you trust. If your school or program has staff onsite who are local residents, use them as a resource. Ask if you could be invited to coffee or for drinks with some of their friends, or if they'll be attending a local festival or event where you could tag along. Your school may also have established programs to help connect students with locals, like a conversation partner program, the opportunity to volunteer in local agencies, or the chance to trade babysitting or tutoring for experiences with local families. If no such program exists, ask if you could start one!

You'll inevitably meet people in public places, and you don't have to shut them down or avoid them just because they're not vetted. But do proceed with caution. If you're alone, keep conversation limited, do not give the person any information they could use to track you down physically, don't let them walk you home, and don't tell them where you live. An email address is enough for them to make contact with you later. If you want to meet again, do it in a public place in daytime, and bring a friend or two with you, and suggest that they do the same. Meeting their friends will give you a better sense of who they are, and bringing your friends will give you a few other people to offer their assessment of the new acquaintance. Continue this pattern until you feel comfortable enough to meet the person alone or in a private location.

112 is the general emergency telephone number for all European Union countries and many other countries in Europe and around the world.

OTHER QUICK SAFETY TIPS

While it's impossible to foresee and prevent any and every circumstance in which you might feel or be unsafe, follow these tips to give yourself the most secure possible foundation:

- Trust your instincts. If something doesn't feel right, it probably isn't.
- Pay attention to your surroundings. Try to see yourself from a

bird's-eye view. Are you calling unnecessary attention to yourself? Are there others around who may be watching, waiting, plotting?

- Pay attention to your personal belongings at all times and in all settings.

- Pay attention to the way people your age dress, and try to match their style to avoid standing out in a crowd.

- Avoid the temptation to take video or photos of dramatic events. You never know when a situation can tip from dramatic to dangerous. Just get yourself to safe ground.

- Always come home with the same number of people you went out with. Leave no one behind.

- If you find yourself alone and away from home after dark, call a taxi. The fare is nothing compared to what it would cost if you were mugged, or worse. Many cities offer discounted taxi fares for women traveling alone after dark, or after a specific time (but you may have to ask in order to get the discount).

- On that note, always have some cash with you in a pocket or shoe, so that you can still get home if your wallet is stolen.

- Don't engage with people who try to give you something to read, or a small trinket, in public places. Many scams start with drawing you in by having you focus on a card explaining that the person is selling something, or taking donations, or with someone tying a bracelet around your wrist and then trying to force you to pay for it, or putting a flower in your hand for the same purpose.

- Do not leave your drink unattended, or drink something you didn't see the bartender pour.

- Have an "escape route." This can be literal or figurative. If you're in a public place, especially after dark, be sure you can see at least two ways to get out of the space you're in, in case of a physical threat, accident, or natural disaster. If you're cornered by someone and need to escape the conversation, have a plan and be willing to act fast, like a glance over the person's shoulder and a quick

"There's my friend!" while you move past him/her. Leave no room for objection.

- Don't do anything that marks you as a tourist or as someone who doesn't know their way around, especially at night or when you're alone. For example, if you're lost, step into a cafe to take a look at your map rather than stopping on the street.

- This seems like a given, but look in the direction in which you are walking. When you're in a group, or fascinated by the new environment around you, you can end up walking while looking at a friend, or a monument, or a sunset. Stop and look, then continue walking. When your attention is not on where you're going, you're at higher risk of being pickpocketed, getting hit by a moving vehicle, causing an accident, or just running into someone who may not appreciate your lack of focus.

- Know what local law enforcement uniforms look like, so that you can identify police (versus someone trying to use a "uniform" to intimidate you).

- Memorize at least one local phone number you can call if you need help (your hotel, a friend's cell, your school's after-hours emergency line), and know the local equivalent of 911 (in most of Europe, **112**).

- This one is worth repeating: Pay attention to your personal belongings at all times and in all settings.

CHAPTER 9

Now It's Time to Thrive

Up to this point, much of this book has focused on pre-departure considerations, and situations you'll face while abroad — what to anticipate, how to react, how to be a good ambassador, how to stay safe. If you've retained even a fraction of what I've shared so far, you're poised to avoid common pitfalls and even teach your fellow travelers a thing or two. **And that's the real mission of this book:** to shorten the learning curve of the predictable, so that you get to spend more of your time abroad thriving, making the best possible use of every last second. So that you get to spend more time learning in rich, deep, extraordinary ways, and less time in the school of hard knocks.

> **My mission in life is not merely to survive, but to thrive; and to do so with some passion, some compassion, some humor, and some style.**
> **-Maya Angelou**

Outfitted with this knowledge, and benefiting from the shared experience of thousands who have gone before you, how do you maximize your study abroad experience? How do you conduct your days so that, when it's time to return home, you're able to look back and say, "I made the most of this. I left nothing on the table."? This chapter aims to get you thinking about how to answer those questions.

KEEP YOUR FOCUS ON THE BIGGER PICTURE

No matter how well you've prepared, there will be days when it seems like the universe is conspiring against you. You might wonder if you will ever feel at home, if you should go home, if you never should have left. When those days happen, just allow whatever thoughts occur to you and whatever feelings come up. Don't judge yourself, but don't make any major decisions, either. Often, getting a good night's sleep and having one small positive experience to change your momentum is enough to wash away any doubts. If "one of those days" stretches out into a few days or longer, try taking a broader view: if you could zoom up to 30,000 feet and see your situation from there, how would it look different? Who is in your environment who can help you? What surrounds you (or is missing from your surroundings) that could offer a possible solution?

WRITE TWO LETTERS

Now, before you leave on this grand adventure abroad, prepare for both the difficult days and the better days by writing yourself two letters. In one letter, imagine that you're a few weeks into your time abroad, you're feeling low, and you aren't having the kind of experience you'd hoped for. Maybe you haven't made good friends, or you have had some health-related challenges, or your living situation is not what you expected. Write a letter offering support, encouragement, and love. Remind yourself that your experience is valuable whether or not it matches your expectations. Remind yourself why you want to study abroad in the first place.

For the better days, when you're coasting along and everything is great, write a second letter. In this letter, challenge yourself to make even more of the experience. You can probably already predict the ways in which you might be complacent, or take the experience for granted. For some, it will be speaking English instead of really trying to improve in the local language. For others, it will be hanging out with Americans too often. Or drinking too much. Or doing the bare minimum academically. Or not trying new foods. In the second letter, remind yourself of the once-in-a-lifetime opportunity you've got. Name the things that might be at the borders of your comfort zone, but that would be fantastic learning opportunities if you'd give them a chance.

Seal these letters, and make sure you know which is which (label the outsides of the envelopes or use a color-coding you'll remember). If you find yourself disappointed or doubtful, open the first letter. If things are going fine, but you're not thriving, open the second. You may never need to open either of them, but knowing they are there will both offer some comfort and keep you inspired to seize every opportunity.

FACE YOUR FEARS

Fear is a funny thing. From a biochemical standpoint, fear exists to save our lives. We're afraid of snakes because they can kill or severely injure us. We're afraid of being alone because a group offers protection. We're afraid of heights, or enclosed spaces, or the dark, because we can easily imagine how each of them could lead to injury or death. But somewhere along the way, some evolutionary wires got crossed, and we started being fearful of things like speaking in public, meeting new people, not being "good enough," looking "stupid," and not being loved. While these situations might be embarrassing or unpleasant or even very sad, they are not life-threatening. Yet we often avoid them as if they are, and thus lose out on the chance to speak in a way that influences someone's life, meet new people, feel more than good enough, look like we're having fun (or, have fun looking stupid), and be open to being loved or appreciated.

Going abroad gives you a chance to reinvent yourself, in a way. Take advantage of that chance. Face your fears! I'm not suggesting that you go BASE jumping or tightrope-walking or engage in anything that actually could kill you. I'm saying, when you're afraid of something, ask yourself what's *really* at stake? What's the worst possible thing that could happen if it doesn't go well, and what's the best outcome if it does? And when will you next have the chance to overcome this fear?

SAY YES

Throughout your days abroad, you'll receive invitations of all kinds. Some of them will appeal to you more than others. But you never know how your openness to one invitation could create a chain reaction of other invitations that end up leading to an opportunity you never could have expected. Have you ever thought of something or someone you appreciate, and worked your way backwards through the connections and choices that brought that person or thing into your life? As in: I met my best friends because we chose the same college, and if I hadn't asked my high school AP biology teacher where she went to college, I wouldn't have even known about this college, and if I hadn't wanted to be like my godfather, who's a doctor, I wouldn't have even taken AP biology, and... so on and so on.

It is possible that during your time abroad, you will have more freedom and more access to opportunity than you've ever had before. But that freedom and opportunity are yours to seize or squander.

So, as long as your safety and health are not at risk, say yes. Every time. And watch what happens.

TRACK PROGRESS

Your time abroad will pass so quickly, and you'll be learning and growing so much every day, that it will be easy to forget how far you've come. If you can keep track of your progress, you'll be able to appreciate it more, and you'll be able to articulate it to others (read: job/internship interviews, parents who paid for the experience, etc.). You don't have to spend an hour writing in a journal every day, although if journaling is your jam, by all means, do that! But there are many ways to keep track of your learning, development, and experiences while abroad.

- Journaling: in the traditional sense, writing what you're doing, how you're feeling, what new insights you've gained

- Constrained journaling: for those who want a quicker model, set a daily limit (3 lines, 5 lines, one paragraph)

- Art journaling: record your progress in mixed media — words, collage, sketches, photos

- Digital journaling: there are lots of great apps to help you do any kind of journaling on your phone, tablet, or laptop

- Map journaling: as mentioned earlier, use free maps of places you visit to record thoughts and experiences directly on them

- Outcome ratings: choose a few areas you want to measure (language proficiency, cultural competency, pushing the edges of your comfort zone, connecting deeply, self-insight), and rank yourself on them from 1-10 every day

- Public/semi-public journaling: create a private Facebook group, a website, or a blog where you share your adventures and learning with others

- Video logging: take a video of yourself at regular intervals and talk about what you're experiencing and learning

In all of these ways of "keeping track," and there are as many more as you can imagine, you'll see the most learning and development if you express your *opinions* and *reactions* to what's happening around you, as opposed to just describing what happened. Write, create, or film in a way that shows your perspective. That's what will change over time and show you how you've grown.

PRACTICE GRATITUDE

Gratitude has become famous in popular culture in the last decade or so, and not without good reason. Hundreds of resources will explain to you the intricacies of how practicing gratitude will change your life, much better than I can do. What I will say is that in my experience, students who consistently expressed their appreciation and gratitude for the opportunity to study abroad, for the support structures around them, and for the world they got to live in each day — they were the ones who seemed to thrive abroad.

CHAPTER 10

Away You Go

By now, you've read pages and pages of specific, practical tips and general advice and guidance about how to make the most of your study abroad experience. It might feel a little overwhelming or intimidating. In fact, if you've read carefully and taken what I've shared to heart, you might actually start to wonder what you've gotten yourself into! If that rings true for you, I invite you to accept this gentle reminder:

> Once in a while it really hits people that they don't have to experience the world in the way they have been told to.
> -Alan Keightley

The subtitle of this book is "A Guide to **Making the Most** of Your Study Abroad Experience," not "A Guide to **Surviving** Your Study Abroad Experience." Hundreds of thousands of American students go abroad every year with little to no preparation, and they survive! Even if you forget or ignore everything you've read, chances are, you'll survive. **The point, however, is not just to survive, but to thrive.** My hope is that having read this book, you'll be better prepared to maximize your experience from day one.

In chapters one through three and nine, I offer many actionable items that you can make your way through to give yourself the strongest foundation and the best launchpad for your term abroad. If you've been reading and absorbing, now is the time to take some action! If you've been taking action all along, great, and now that you've almost finished the book, it might be beneficial to circle back around to the questions in chapter one:

- Who am I?
- What do I want?
- What is important to me?
- What do I value?

Perhaps you've had some reactions to issues that were introduced, or to something you learned, in the more practically-oriented chapters. Those reactions — excitement, resistance, fear, anticipation, uncertainty, wonder, the possibilities are unlimited — may highlight additional answers to the Basic Questions, or areas where you thought you knew the answer and now want to reconsider. I would even recommend re-reading the first chapter, now that you've heard about how the study abroad experience might look at a much more granular level. Answer the questions again and notice what, if anything, has changed. What new clarity do you have about how you want your term abroad to look? What questions do you have, that you might not have even known to ask before? Who can you call on as a consultant or advisor as you enter the final stages of preparation?

START WITH THE ENDING

One really effective way to stay connected to your big-picture goals and take daily actions to support them: imagine that you're at the end, you've finished the experience, and look back on what "happened" to get you there. Consider questions like:

- As a final exam for one of your classes, you're asked to write a summary of what you learned and how you grew through your study abroad term. What do you say about yourself?

- You inevitably faced some stumbling blocks, and maybe even had some distinctly negative experiences. What perspective will you take regarding those situations?

- You get home and people say things like, "Wow, you seem so much more [insert adjective here] than when you left!" What is it that they'll notice about you? How will you describe what you learned about yourself?

When you think about your answers to these questions, you don't have to know what's going to happen while you're abroad, or what your environment will be like, where you'll go or what you'll see. Regardless of the details, the critical question is, who will you be? How will you show up?

In preparing to write this book, I asked some of my former students what advice they'd give to others who were preparing to study abroad. While they had diverse (and sometimes, conflicting!) responses about specific things like what to bring or where to go, many of their answers had a common theme: *slow down and be in the present moment.* The time will go by faster than you can imagine. While it's healthy to maintain some connections to home, and some habits from home that support your well-being, embrace that you have access to a completely new place in the world, and a completely unknown side of yourself. Focus on appreciating that opportunity and what it means to the rest of your life, and you'll be much more able to let the small stuff slide, and see the value in every experience. Stop, often, to take a deep breath and be fully aware of where you are, what you're doing, and who you're being.

My hope for you is that you will be fully prepared for departure. That you will take the time to explore the questions presented in this book, so that — more than just having planned well — you will have learned and practiced essential skills, and begun the process of personal evolution (one that will continue to unfold while you're abroad, and for the rest of your life) before you ever get on that plane.

My wish for you is that your study abroad experience is the richest, most profound, deepest, most exciting, fulfilling, meaningful, educational, and life-affirming experience it can possibly be. That on the last day of your term abroad, you're able to say without hesitation or qualification, "I did it. I arrived prepared, and brave, and open. I took advantage of every opportunity I was given, and I created some of my own. I played all out, I made the most of the experience, and I have no regrets."

Workbook

To get your copy of the companion workbook, mentioned throughout this book, go to shelleystory.com/workbook.

About the Author

Shelley Story has spent two decades helping college students overcome challenges and seize opportunities. After completing a master's degree in Student Personnel in Higher Education at the University of Georgia, she held positions in residence life and dean's offices at Whittier College, American University, TCU, and Gonzaga. A certified professional coach, she loves a creative question.

For nine years, Shelley developed and managed the student life division of a study abroad institute in Florence, Italy, where she created programs to help students thrive. She also waged war on bedbugs, listened intently, and offered homemade treats and free hugs. She traveled about 800 days in those nine years, with student groups as small as 12 and as large as 195, to 24 countries on three continents. She can give you a walking tour of several European cities without a map, but still has a hard time packing in just a carry-on.

Shelley lives in Austin, Texas. When she's not coaching, writing, or traveling to speak to college students, you'll find her with a crochet hook, paintbrush, or cookie cutter in hand. She's on Twitter at @shelleystory.

To my mind, the greatest reward and luxury of travel is to be able to experience everyday things as if for the first time, to be in a position in which almost nothing is so familiar it is taken for granted.

-*Bill Bryson*

Made in the USA
San Bernardino, CA
05 August 2016